THE HISTORY OF
NORTH AMERICAN RAIL

THE HISTORY OF
NORTH AMERICAN
RAIL

Christopher Chant

CHARTWELL
BOOKS, INC.

Published in 2005 by
Chartwell Books, Inc.
A division of Book Sales, Inc.
114 Northfield Avenue
Edison, New Jersey 08837, U.S.A.

ISBN 0-7858-1455-8

Printed in China by Sino
Publishing House Limited

CONTENTS

CHAPTER ONE
AMERICAN BEGINNINGS
(1828–1861)

By the start of the 19th century, the United States of America had acquired its independence from the United Kingdom and secured itself internally against insurgencies by the Native American population. The population of the country was beginning to grow rapidly, and already evident were the first waves of the westward expansion that was eventually to extend the U.S.A. right across the North American continent. The primary driving force in this first tide of expansion was the combination of high taxation, costly land, and the rigidity of the social order, exacerbated in the southern states by increasing impoverishment of the soil and the spread of plantations. As a result, swelling numbers of Americans looked to the virgin lands west of the current extent of civilization and began to look for new lives in these areas.

The first stage of this westward expansion was based on land routes, mostly in the form of new roads, then

scarcely more than tracks hacked through the woods and forests, along the three main axes from Boston and the rest of New England along the Mohawk valley to Lake Erie, from Philadelphia and Baltimore across the Appalachian mountains to the valley of the Ohio river, and from the cities and plantations of Virginia and North Carolina to Nashville and Louisville in the valleys of the Tennessee and Ohio rivers respectively. From these areas to points farther to the west, it was rivers and lakes that provided the main routes to the west, and in the first 25 years of the 19th century new routes were developed to facilitate this westward movement and connect the newly settled regions to the rest of the U.S.A. for trading purposes. By 1818 the paved National Road had been completed to Wheeling on the banks of the Ohio river, in 1825 the Erie Canal was opened for business between the Hudson river and Lake Erie across the northern part of New York state, and up the rivers from the south paddle-wheel steamers were starting to reach the fertile plains of Ohio, Indiana and Illinois.

The pioneers of the westward drive were generally farming families and those who depended on farming for their own ways of life. Soon, great new areas of fertile land were under cultivation, yielding quantities of grain and other produce far too large for local consumption. By one of the inevitable coincidences of fortune, however, exactly the same period was seeing the rapid growth of industrialization in the north-eastern states of the U.S.A. and the general replacement of conventional farming by cotton planting in the southern states. The solution, immediately obvious to the merchant organizations in the east coast states, was an exchange of western food for eastern manufactured goods in a process that would yield the merchants fat profits. The only problem was transportation, or rather the lack of it, by which this exchange could be undertaken in a manner that would be reliable, timely, cost-effective and therefore profitable. The current transport network was clearly inadequate to meet these requirements: the roads across the mountains between the original states and the new lands to the west were too slow for large-scale transportation of grain, and the route down the rivers to New Orleans, followed by a sea journey through the Gulf of Mexico and around Florida to the ports of the eastern seaboard was slow and tortuous, and also involved travel through climatic regions likely to damage the merchandise.

The Erie Canal was the first major attempt to overcome the transport hurdle in the north, and was largely successful in creating great reductions in the financial and time burdens of transport. The opening of the Erie Canal was of considerable importance to New York, lying as it does at the mouth of the Hudson river on the eastern seaboard, and the city soon became the most important

AMERICAN BEGINNINGS (1828–1861)

trading centre of the region. The reason for this growth in New York's significance and affluence was readily discernible to the major players in other north-eastern port cities, who in short order demanded comparable links to the interior. In the short term, these links were also envisaged as canals, but it soon became clear that there were major geographical problems associated with the task of building, or rather driving, canals through the mountains lying between the other eastern port cities and the burgeoning new hinterlands of the U.S.A. Nevertheless, some canals were planned and built but the difficulties and basic inefficiency of systems that fought against rather than cooperated with nature can be seen in the case of the Pennsylvanian city of Philadelphia: the city persuaded the state administration to create a system of canals that reached Pittsburgh in the western part of the state by 1834; but to cross the mountain ridge required goods to be hauled 10 miles (16km) up a series of inclined planes before coasting down the other side and continuing their journey. Another canal was the Chesapeake & Ohio, started in 1827 as a joint project by Baltimore in Maryland and Washington, D.C. More important by far, however, was the launch in the same year of an entirely new concept that was to replace the canal and revolutionize transport in the U.S.A.

Spurred by the limited but real success of the first pioneering British railways, the concept of the railway soon crossed the Atlantic to the U.S.A., where the idea of

transport capable of moving at a steady three or four times the 4mph (6.5km/h) possible by canal boats was immediately attractive. The first U.S. railroad to launch services was the Baltimore & Ohio Railroad that began operation with horse-drawn carriages in the course of April 1827. The first steam locomotives did not arrive in the U.S.A. until 1829, when the distinction of being the first steam locomotive to run on an American railroad, in this instance the Delaware & Hudson Railroad, was secured by the *Stourbridge Lion*, one of four locomotives bought in the U.K. and shipped across the Atlantic. The locomotive was too heavy for the rails, however, for these rails were of iron-plated wooden construction and the Delaware & Hudson had therefore to return to horsepower for several more years.

The Baltimore & Ohio Railroad planned a route extending from the port city of Baltimore at the head of Chesapeake Bay to the Ohio river, where the rail route would link with the river network that carried most of the trade in the interior. This was a distance of 380 miles (612km), requiring the traverse of a major mountain range, more than ten times the length of any railroad previously attempted. The process of constructing the railroad, by men without any real experience of the demands of railroad construction and operation, was pursued with a determination of the type that came to be seen as particularly American. Engineers of the U.S. Army were called in to undertake the survey on which the route would be

based, and this began along the Patapsco river before heading across country to reach and then follow the line of the Potomac river through the Caboctin mountains. It was on 4 July 1828 that work on the new line started, and within three years profits from horse-drawn traffic on the first few miles of track encouraged the Baltimore & Ohio's board of directors to take a bold new step in offering prizes of $4,000 and $3,500 for the best steam locomotives delivered by 1 June 1831: the engines were to turn the scales at not more than $3^{1}/_{2}$ tons and prove themselves able to haul a 15-ton train at 15mph (24km/h).

By this time there had already appeared in the U.S.A. a number of steam locomotives. The first of these was a small engine made by Colonel John Stevens, an early American protagonist of the railroad, and trialled on a small track in his back yard. The first commercial locomotives, however, were units imported from the U.K. to the order placed by Horatio Allen for the Delaware & Hudson Canal company. As might be inferred from its full name, the Delaware & Hudson was involved in the canal-construction business, in this instance linking Rondout in New York state with the Carbondale mines in north-western Pennsylvania. The last 16 miles (26km) of the planned route from Honesdale were so fraught with difficulties for the canal builder, however, that the company's chief engineer, John B. Jervis, began to consider the possibility of replacing the canal on this part of the

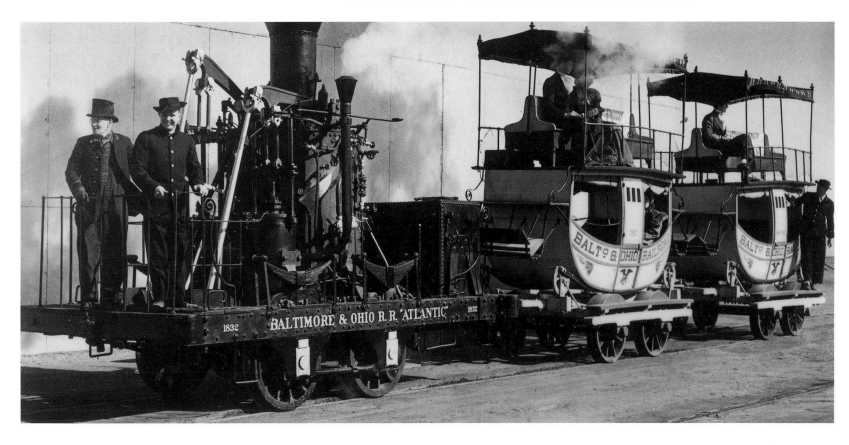

OPPOSITE
This reconstruction of Mohawk & Hudson's locomotive, DeWitt Clinton, *was manufactured in 1893.*

LEFT
Another view of the locomotive Atlantic *of the Baltimore & Ohio Railroad.*

route with a railroad. Allen travelled to England to buy iron rails and any locomotive engines he thought might fit the bill: the first of these latter, named *America* and manufactured by Robert Stephenson, arrived in New York in January 1829. Allen ordered another three locomotives from the Stourbridge firm of Foster, Rastrick. Two of these, named *Hudson* and *Delaware*, were lost in a fire in the shed in which they were being stored after their arrival at Rondout, but the third unit, named *Stourbridge Lion*, was evaluated at the West Point Foundry in New York City after its arrival in May

1829, and then shipped to Honesdale. On 8 August of that year the *Stourbridge Lion* was readied for its first trip: given the difficult nature of the journey, over a twisting route and with the wooden rails somewhat distorted by warping, Allen opted to make the inaugural trip on his own. The new locomotive set off along the 500-ft (152-m) length of straight track that led into a sharp curve and thence a trestle bridge. Many believed that the locomotive would fail to round the first curve, but the *Stourbridge Lion* encountered no difficulty with the task, steamed over the bridge, and then

proceeded a further 3 miles (4.8km) along the track before Allen halted it and then returned it to its starting point.

So ended the first locomotive journey in America. Allen may be regarded as fortunate on this initial outing, for in its following career the *Stourbridge Lion* suffered a number of derailments before being relegated to service as a stationary boiler in a foundry at Carbondale. The historically important locomotive was then rebuilt for the Chicago Railway Exposition of 1884, and was finally preserved for posterity by the Smithsonian Institution.

A replica of the Best Friend of Charleston. *The original hauled the first passenger train in 1836 for the South Carolina Canal & Railroad.*

Meanwhile, the Baltimore & Ohio Railroad had begun railroad services, and in 1830 one of its shareholders, Peter Cooper, built a locomotive that has a secure niche in U.S. history as the first American-built steam locomotive. Intended only to demonstrate the capabilities of the locomotive, the *Tom Thumb* massed only 1 ton, and its working innards included boiler tubes made out of gun barrels and a fan powered by one of the axles to create the draft for the fire. Despite its experimental nature, though, on 28 August 1830 the *Tom Thumb* hauled a coach carrying 36 passengers along a route of some 15 miles (24km) from Baltimore to Ellicott Mills at speeds of up to 18mph (29km/h). On the *Tom Thumb*'s return journey, the locomotive was challenged to a race by a horse-drawn rail car on a parallel track, and while the locomotive initially outperformed the horse-drawn car, the latter won the race after the *Tom Thumb*'s fire died as a result of slippage in the belt driving the draft fan.

Even so, the basic superiority of the steam locomotive over the horse-drawn car was plain for all to see. In the competition mentioned above, the only contender that met all the requirements of the specification, and was therefore declared the winner, was the *York*, designed by Phineas Davis, a watchmaker of Philadelphia. The Baltimore & Ohio Railroad then ordered 20 examples of an improved version of the *York*: known as Grasshoppers, through their combination

bogies. On 25 December 1830 the *Best Friend of Charleston* was the locomotive that launched the U.S.A.'s first steam-hauled regular schedule of services on the Charleston & Hamburg company's 6 miles (9.65km) of track.

West Point Foundry was now gaining a good reputation for its locomotives, and accordingly began to gather orders from other railroads. In 1831 the company delivered a locomotive, designed by John B. Jervis and named the *DeWitt Clinton* after the governor of New York, to the

LEFT
The locomotive Tom Thumb, *built by Peter Cooper for the Baltimore & Ohio Railroad in 1829.*

BELOW
Replica of the Best Friend of Charleston, *built for use on the South Carolina Railroad.*

of vertical boilers driving the wheels by means of rocking beams, the locomotives were able to haul 50-ton trains along the track of the railroad's winding route. Many of the locomotives remained in service for up to half a century, the last unit being retired only in 1893.

The obvious potential of the steam locomotive had already caught the attention of other engineering companies, several of which had begun preliminary work on the design and manufacture of such units. During 1830 the West Point Foundry made the *Best Friend of Charleston* for the Charleston & Hamburg Railroad, whose track was currently being built by the new employer of Allen, the South Carolina Canal & Railroad company. On

its first run the *Best Friend of Charleston* broke a wheel, but on its second attempt attained a speed of 20mph (32km/h) while hauling a train with 40 of the company's men on board.

The *Best Friend of Charleston* was destroyed by a boiler explosion only a few months later, but before this occurrence had been complemented by another locomotive manufactured by the West Point Foundry. Named *West Point*, this second locomotive had a horizontal boiler rather than the *Best Friend of Charleston*'s vertical boiler; a third locomotive from the same company in the same year was the *South Carolina*, which had two boilers, each driving one centreline cylinder on separate four-wheel

ABOVE
The Tom Thumb, *built by Peter Cooper. On 28 August 1830 this experimental engine hauled the directors of Baltimore & Ohio from Baltimore, Maryland to Ellicott Mills to become the first locomotive to pull a load of passengers.*

ABOVE RIGHT
The DeWitt Clinton *was built for the Mohawk & Hudson Railroad and made the 17-mile (27-km) trip from Albany to Schenectady in less than an hour in August 1931.*

Mohawk & Hudson Railroad established by the financial interests of Albany and Schenectady businessmen as a means of linking Albany with the eastern end of the Erie Canal. In the following year, the *Experiment*, which was another Jervis design for the Mohawk & Hudson, proved that the West Point Foundry was developing along the right technical lines, for this 4-2-0 unit revealed none of the instability that had afflicted the company's earlier locomotives. This instability was a direct consequence of the poor tracks on which the locomotives had to operate, for the tracks transmitted their uneven and twisting nature to the locomotive as the latter were rigidly-framed four-wheel units. The problem was solved by the

introduction of a three-point suspension arrangement: the axle for the main driving wheels was carried by two bearings, one at each end, and now the front of the locomotive was supported via a single centreline pivot by a four-wheel bogie. The system proved efficacious in allowing the front wheels to conform to variations in the track, and this type of 4-2-0 layout was soon copied by other locomotive builders.

One of these other companies was located in Philadelphia and headed by Matthias Baldwin, whose starting point was a study of the *John Bull*, a Stephenson Planet-type locomotive imported in 1831 by Robert L. Stevens for the Camden & Amboy Railroad of New Jersey. Baldwin

built a similar 2-2-0 locomotive, the *Old Ironsides*, for the Philadelphia, Germanstown & Norristown Railroad, but Baldwin was a quick learner and his next locomotive, the *E. L. Miller* for the Charleston & Hamburg, was of the 4-2-0 configuration with a haystack firebox. A basically similar arrangement was used by another Philadelphia builder, William Norris, in his *George Washington* of 1836. The concept was further developed by Henry Campbell in a 4-4-0 locomotive he designed and manufactured for the Philadelphia, Germanstown & Norristown during 1836. Two years later, though, the major breakthrough in this field came with Joseph Harrison's patent for a system of equalizing beams to support the coupled

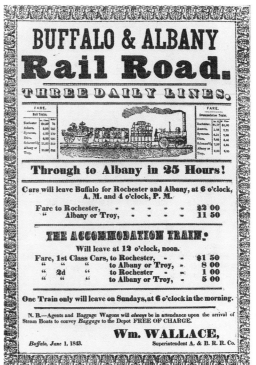

ABOVE
The locomotive Hercules, *built by Garret & Eastwich of Philadelphia for the Beaver Meadow Railroad in 1837.*

LEFT
Poster advertising the first through trains between Buffalo and Albany in 1843.

ABOVE LEFT
The David & Gartner locomotive Grasshopper *of the Baltimore & Ohio Railroad, 1864.*

FAR LEFT
The Pioneer *of the Chicago & North Western Railroad.*

Baltimore & Ohio's replica of 4-2-0 Lafayette No. 13, built in 1937 at its Mount Clare shops. The original was in operation in 1837.

driving wheels. In combination with the pivoted leading bogie, this type of suspension made it possible for all the wheels to remain in contact with the track despite the latter's variations.

The construction of these and other locomotives was, of course, a function of the growth of the American railroad industry, which had been received with great commercial and social enthusiasm, albeit for a number of different reasons in different parts of the U.S.A. It was the

success of the Erie Canal that had inspired the Baltimore & Ohio, together with other railroads in north-eastern parts of the country, to enter the railroad arena, while the motivation of ports such as Richmond, Charleston and Savannah in the south-eastern states was the desirability of linking to trading areas coming into existence farther to the west, as the practice of cotton planting extended in that direction. The establishment of the South Carolina Railroad to Hamburg on

the Savannah river was an effort to divert river trade to Hamburg and thus away from Savannah; after the South Carolina Railroad had been finished, the Charleston financial interests invested in the Georgia Railroad so that its route could be extended to Athens and Atlanta. Savannah's response to these encroachments on its trading position was the Central Railroad of Georgia, backed by the state administration, extending toward Macon, and the Monroe Railroad

linking Macon and Atlanta. The other major commercial centre of the area was Richmond, which planned to use its canal to Lynchburg as the base on which the Lynchburg & New River Railroad would be built with the final object of reaching the Ohio river.

The new states in the west, which had initially been content to let eastern interests build the railroads that would boost both areas' prosperity, were not faced with the problems of dealing with the ever-increasing quantities of grain and other produce that came with the introduction of more farmers and more intensive cultivation. It was now clearly the time to improve communications within the western states. Once more, it was the presence of the Erie Canal that constituted the first impetus for much of the western states' first direct involvement in the creation of more canals and then railroads. Ohio, Indiana, Illinois and Michigan all launched major programmes for new canals: these were intended to link existing canal and river routes with the Great Lakes, in the process freeing the farmers of these states from the need to ship their produce down the Mississippi and other rivers to New Orleans. It was appreciated that a programme of canal construction on this scale would be very expensive in capital terms, but it was expected that the greater profit margins provided by the simplified movement of produce to the east would soon pay off the required loans.

During the 1830s the canal-building

LEFT
the 1831 York, *by Phineas Davis of York, Pennsylvania, winning Baltimore & Ohio's $4,000 first prize. It hauled the York Express from Baltimore to Ellicott Mills, making the trip in one hour*

BELOW LEFT
The Sundusky 4-2-0-type locomotive, built for the Mad River & Lake Erie Railroad by Rogers Locomotive Works in 1837.

RIGHT
Baltimore & Ohio Railroad 'camelbacks' at Martinsburg, Virginia with, in the foreground, a coal train bound for Baltimore. 1858.

BELOW RIGHT
A passenger train of the Illinois Central Railroad. 1856.

OPPOSITE
A 4-4-0 locomotive of the Chicago & Eastern Illinois Railroad, 1854.

programme was modified to allow for the introduction of railroads which could clearly enhance the overall capabilities of the system to a marked degree. However, the rate of construction did not match the scope of the programme; the rate at which interest began to grow on the vast sums borrowed by the state governments to finance the programme soon overtook current or even expected revenues and in 1837 caused a financial crisis and then an economic depression that saddled the states with huge debts but little to show for the effort.

In Ohio two railroads, the Little Miami and the Mad River & Lake Erie, were conceived as the means of connecting Springfield with Cincinnati and the Ohio river to the south and with Sandusky on the lake to the north: a law of 1837, laying it down that the state would buy one-third of the stock of any railroad which had raised the other two-thirds of its capital requirement, saw $3,000,000 disappear into the hands of 40 non-existent builders, and was repealed in 1840. Millions more dollars spent by Indiana resulted in a few miles of preparatory work for railroads to connect Madison with Lafayette and New Albany with Crawfordsville before they were sold. In 1837, Illinois agreed to construct the Illinois Central Railroad from Cairo in the south to Galena in the north-west, as well as the Northern Cross and Southern Cross Railroads to provide east/west links: by 1842 only half the Northern Cross Railroad, from Quincy to Springfield, had been completed. Farther

BELOW
Chicago's first railroad station, built in 1848. The railroad's president, armed with a telescope, could keep watch from a tower to spot the smoke from inbound trains, so that he could announce their arrival.

BELOW
Chicago's first railroad station, built in 1848. The railroad's president, armed with a telescope, could keep watch from a tower to spot the smoke from inbound trains, so that he could announce their arrival.

BELOW RIGHT
This two-storey building replaced Galena & Chicago Union's first building in 1853. It was subsequently destroyed by fire in 1871.

north, the Erie & Kalamazoo Railroad, which was the first to be established in the west, had set off from Toledo and reached Adrian by 1836; after it had become a state in 1837, and in the process gained a freer hand in the ordering of its own affairs, Michigan planned a network of northern, central and southern railroads: as in so many other cases, the state raised and disbursed vast sums, but the guarantor banks collapsed, and work was halted in 1842.

What was now in effect a railroad mania was just as prevalent farther to the south, where once again cities felt that the completion of railroads to other cities in

the area, and also to the east and west, would free them from their current commercial shackles to river and/or maritime trade routes. For example, the Louisville, Cincinnati & Charleston Railroad was launched by the states of South Carolina, Tennessee and Kentucky, but construction was halted in 1839 by lack of adequate financing and also inter-state arguments concerning the route. In another area, the plan for a series of short railroads, intended to provide a link between Memphis in Tennessee and Charleston in South Carolina, comprised only 8 miles (12.9km) of track when the 1837 panic halted further construction.

Vicksburg in Mississippi planned a route eastward to Charleston, but only the first link to Jackson had been completed by 1840, when the rest of the plan folded. North/south lines were proposed from Mobile to Chattanooga and from New Orleans to Nashville, but these too were abandoned after only small sections of the routes had been completed.

In a short time, therefore, the railroad mania became an antipathy among members of a public now faced with financial problems and evidence that very large sums of money, raised by taxation to pay for loans, had been squandered. Thus 1837 marked a short-term turning point in

Some of the most striking 4-4-0 locomotives were designed by William Mason, this example being a unit built in 1857 for the Baltimore & Ohio Railroad.

the development of American railroads as state authorities became wary of asking for further investment and construction programmes foundered for lack of financing.

Even so, these and the other state-backed railroads of the 1830s became the blocks on which later construction began; but while the foundations had been built with public finance, the completion of the programmes was left to private finance, which ultimately reaped any profits. This process also had a major effect on the development of the eastern part of the U.S.A., for there were few men in the southern states with the capital and/or the inclination to invest in railroads; therefore, the required financing of the new railroads became the province of men who had made their money in the industrialization of the northern states and were then in the position to take the profits back to the north. In effect, this resulted in a continued impoverishment of the south vis-à-vis the north.

The Baltimore & Ohio Railroad had reached Cumberland, little more than mid-way on its way to its ultimate objective, during the course of 1842, but the railroad managed to maintain its existence through the depression and in 1848 began further construction work so that the line had reached Wheeling on the Ohio river by 1853. The Baltimore & Ohio also planned a spur to Pittsburgh in Pennsylvania, and this so concerned financiers in Philadelphia, currently Pittsburgh's primary trading partner, that in 1847 they launched the Pennsylvania Railroad, which linked the two cities by 1853.

Meanwhile, the Mohawk & Hudson in New York state had been supplemented from 1836 by the Utica & Schenectady Railroad, and during the 1840s links between towns on the Erie Canal created a rail route joining Albany with Buffalo on the southern shore of Lake Erie. Then in 1851 and 1852 the completion of the Hudson River and New York & Harlem Railroads, respectively, joined Albany with New York down the valley of the Hudson river. In 1853, a bout of very sensible consolidation in this nest of small operators saw the merger of these small railroads into the New York Central Railroad, whose lines covered the area between New York and Lake Erie to the very considerable advantage of passengers, who did not need to change trains as they had when connecting via a number of different operators. At much the same time, but in the southern half of New York state, the New York & Erie Railroad was re-formed after its bankruptcy during the depression had ended its first existence from 1832, and by 1851 had a service linking Piermont on the Hudson river to Dunkirk on Lake Erie.

By the middle of the 19th century, it was clear to the major railroad companies that they had to create viable links to the railroads springing up in the west if the steamboat operators of the Mississippi and other rivers were not to gain a stranglehold of trade into and out of these states. The key area in this thinking was that to the west of the Ohio river, and it was the influx of financial resources from the east that now allowed a resumption of railroad building after the problems of the late 1830s and the 1840s. First off the mark was the Mad River & Lake Erie Railroad, revived in 1846 and reaching Sandusky on the Ohio shore of Lake Erie within a mere two years. At the same time, the completion of a line between Sandusky and the Ohio Canal paved the way for new railroads, completed in 1852, connecting Cleveland, another port city on the southern shore of Lake Erie and a commercial rival to Sandusky, with the inland cities of Cincinnati and Columbus. In 1853 there opened the westward extensions to Cleveland and Toledo of the New York Central and Erie systems, and over this short period the Pennsylvania Railroad was extended westward from Pittsburgh in the direction of Chicago.

Lying on the southern tip of Lake Michigan, Chicago was a city of rapidly growing commercial significance, a fact signalled by the establishment of the Chicago & Galena, the Chicago, Burlington & Quincy, and the Chicago & Rock Island Railroads, all of which fanned out to the west of Chicago. Most important of all, these developments were the start of renewed work on the Illinois Central, which was now schemed as the railroad link connecting Cairo, lying on the junction of the Ohio and Mississippi rivers in the south of Illinois, with Chicago and Galena in the north. The links with Galena and Chicago were finished in 1855

CHICAGO, IOWA & NEBRASKA R. ROAD

Time Table No. 2.

To go into effect Sunday, April 15th, 1860.

For the Government and Information of Employees only.

TRAINS WEST			TRAINS EAST	
2	**1**	STATIONS.	**1**	**2**
PASS.	FREIGHT		PASS.	FREIGHT
P. M.	A. M.		A. M.	P. M.
4:05	8:30	CLINTON, - - -	10:45	4:00
4:20	8:50	Camanche, -	10:32	3:40
4:35	9:10	Low Moor, - -	10:20	3:25
4:45	9:25	Ramessa, - - -	10:10	3:10
5:05	**9:50**	De Witt, - - -	**9:50**	2:45
5:20	10:10	G'd Mound, -	9:30	2:20
5:40	10:30	Calmas, - - - -	9:13	1:55
5:50	10:45	Yankee Run,	9:04	1:40
6:05	11:05	Louden, - - -	8:52	1:25
6:25	11:35	Onion Grove,	8:31	1:00
6:55	**12:20**	Me'chsville,	8:03	**12:20**
7:15	1:05	Lisbon, - - - -	7:42	11:50
7:23	1:20	Mt. Vernon, -	7:36	11:25
7:45	1:45	Bertram, - -	7:15	10:50
8:15	2:25	Cedar Rapids,	6:45	10:10
P. M.	P. M.		A. M.	A. M.

Trains will meet and pass at Stations indicated by full face figures.

Train No. 2 West and No. 1 East have the right to the road against all other Trains for *one hour* after their own time at any Station as per table. After that time the right of the road belongs to the other Trains.

Train No. 2 East has the right to the road against No. 1 West for *one hour* after their own time at any Station, as per table. After that time the right of the road belongs to No. 1 West.

M. SMITH, Sup't.

and 1856 respectively. What was notably interesting about this renewed effort was the way in which it was financed: the state gave the Illinois Central land grant sections, alternating on each side of the line, for sale to realize the money needed for construction: the concept of land grants was destined to become a major factor in the financing of future railroads. The completion of these new links was just as important within the context of the shaping of the U.S.A.'s patterns of trade and passenger movement. The western states were now connected by rail to the ports of the north-western states rather than by water to the ports of the south.

The ending of the depression and the resumption of interest in railroad construction also meant that work was restarted on a number of the southern railroads, albeit at a comparatively slow pace. The number of railroad links connecting the Mississippi, Gulf of Mexico, and ports of the eastern seaboard with the leading cities of the U.S.A.'s inland regions, began to grow, but oddly enough no real attempt was made to create any significant links with the railroad systems of the north. The situation was also made more inconvenient by the fact that the majority of the southern railroads were built to the 60-in (1.52-m) gauge, first adopted by the Charleston & Hamburg, rather than the 56-in (1.42-m) gauge that was common but certainly not universal among the northern railroads.

These latter continued to forge ahead

LEFT
An Easter 1860 timetable for the Chicago, Iowa & Nebraska Railroad.

to the west during the 1850s. A notable event, taking place in 1854, was the arrival of the Rock Island Railroad on the eastern border of Illinois at the bank of the Mississippi river. This was next to be spanned by a bridge based on Rock Island, which had given the railroad it name and, against the vehement opposition of steamboat operators fearing the loss of their livelihoods, the bridge was completed to take the railroad over the river to Davenport in Iowa. Only a short time after this, the wooden bridge itself was burned to destruction after a steamboat had struck one of its supports. The result was a series of legal actions whose upshot in the U.S. Supreme Court was a decision that the railroads had as much right to bridge rivers as the steamboats to ply them.

Henry Farnam, president of the Rock Island Railroad, was already looking farther to the west. He established the Mississippi & Missouri Railroad to take railroad transport across Iowa. Other operators followed suit: the Missouri Pacific Railroad departed from St. Louis in Missouri toward Kansas City on the border between Missouri and Kansas, and the Chicago & North Western Railroad drove forward over the Mississippi at Clinton in Iowa toward Council Bluffs on the Missouri river. In the event, these two operators lost out to a Missouri-based company, the Hannibal & St. Joseph Railroad, which secured federal land grants and began work in 1851: early in 1859 sections of the railroad being build

simultaneously from the east and west came together.

The acceleration in the rate of railroad construction is attested by the figures: in 1840 the U.S.A. had 2,800 miles (4505km) of railroad, by 1850 the figure had increased to 9,000 miles (14485km), but only 10 years later still, in 1860, the figure had soared to 30,000 miles (48280km) or more. In terms of trading patterns the changes were equally dramatic, relegating New Orleans from its position as the country's leading port for export trade. Resulting from the U.K.'s 1846 repeal of the Corn Laws, allowing the import of wheat, as well as the opening of a host of new railroad connections, New York was now the U.S.A.'s primary port for the export trade.

Essentially coinciding with the completion of this first main phase of the U.S.A.'s development of its railroad system was the advent of the steam locomotive that was to remain unaltered for the following half of the century and thus to serve as the workhorse of American railroads until the end of the 19th century. This did not spring into being directly, but was the result of evolution that saw the development of a number of less successful contenders characterized by different wheel arrangements. In 1842, for example, Baldwin introduced an eight-coupled freight locomotive, initially for the Central Railroad of Georgia and the Philadelphia & Reading Railroad: this interesting locomotive combined greater tractive

effort by adding more driving wheels and improved flexibility to cater for track irregularities by mounting the two front pairs of driving wheels on flexible beams and using ball-and-socket couplings to the two rear pairs of driving wheels mounted in a rigid frame. The most common, indeed the virtually universal, locomotive came to be known as the American type, and this had a 4-4-0 arrangement with its leading bogie and equalized driving wheels offering the best possible mix of tractive power and flexibility. The configuration was created in the 1830s, and was soon developed into its increasingly standard form by the addition of a wide firebox for burning wood, the standard fuel of the early days; the rear of the boiler was adjusted to a conical shape to fit the firebox; a single large head lamp, substantial balloon stack, chimney, sand box and bell were disposed along the top of the boiler and smokebox; and a cab at the rear was added to protect the engineer and fireman.

This became the standard locomotive of the railroads that conquered the vastness of the U.S.A., from the border with Canada to the shores of the Gulf of Mexico, and from the eastern shore along the Atlantic Ocean to the western shore along the Pacific. This last became a deciding element in the development of the American railroad system; the increasingly common appearance of the word 'Pacific' in the names of railroad companies during the 1850s was a sure sign that American operators had their

OPPOSITE
Baltimore & Ohio's 1848 Memnon, *built by the New Castle Delaware Foundry & Machine Company, hauled men and material during the Civil War, when it was called* War Horse. *Note the inclined cylinder and piston.*

sights fixed on creating a transcontinental east/west link right across a country that had now spread to California on the shores of the Pacific.

By 1846, when the U.S.A. gained California and Oregon from Mexico and the U.K. respectively, there were already proposals for a transcontinental railroad link from sea to shining sea. Some of these proposals were fanciful, to say the least, but there were also a number of more feasible suggestions. Among the latter was the 1845 plan of Asa Whitney, a New England trader, who saw in the transcontinental railroad link the best way of opening up trade with the Far East: Whitney proposed to the federal authorities that they grant him a belt of land some 60-miles (97-km) wide between the Great Lakes and Oregon, and that in return he would built a railroad. There was strong opposition, mainly from those in regions which wanted the route to start from their bailiwicks, and in 1948 a bill to grant Whitney's concept approval was defeated by only a relatively narrow margin.

There was nothing that could halt the public sentiment in favour of a transcontinental railroad, and during 1853 the U.S. Congress issued instructions that the U.S. Army was to undertake a survey of possible routes. The army proposed four routes, two in the north and two in the south. The former extended from Lake Superior to Portland in Oregon and through South Pass to San Francisco in California, while the latter ran along the

Red River or through southern Texas to southern California. Then Stephen A. Douglas, an Illinois senator who had been heavily involved in the implementation of land grants for the Illinois Central Railroad, proposed that three routes should be followed as one in the north, one in the centre to San Francisco, and one in the south from Texas to southern California. Other proposals were made by the backers of the Leavenworth, Pawnee & Western Railroad, a company which had no track but which had gained rights to

large tracts of Native American land in Kansas on its planned route west from the Missouri border, and by the backers of the Hannibal & St. Joseph Railroad, who wanted to extend their line west along the route pioneered by the Pony Express mail service that had been launched from St. Joseph in 1860.

While these and others were interested in the extension of the U.S.A.'s eastern railroads to the west coast, there was a growing belief in the west that the time was ripe for a network to be extended

eastward. A leading light in this movement was Theodore Judah, a Connecticut engineer located in California to oversee the construction of a short railway linking Sacramento and the mining area near Placerville, Colorado. Judah's thinking caught the attention of businessmen such as Charles Crocker, Mark Hopkins, Collis P. Huntington and Leland Stanford. In 1860 Judah was unsuccessful in securing approval from the federal authorities, and the four California businessmen formed a consortium to promote Judah's idea, initially with a survey to find a route better than that suggested by the army's survey teams. Judah, Crocker, Huntington and Stanford looked at the Sierra Nevada region in the summer of 1860 to decide the route of their planned railroad, mapping a line through the Donner Pass that trimmed more than 100 miles (160km) from the army survey teams' planned route, and would also provide a service to the valley of the Carson river, where new mines were coming into production. The next step was the securing of federal approval, and with it federal subsidies. In 1861 the consortium created the Central Pacific Railroad of California with funds of $200,000, and Huntington departed to join Judah in Washington to press their case.

LEFT
The Thatcher Perkins, *No. 117 of the Baltimore & Ohio Railroad, c. 1860.*

BELOW LEFT
An engraving of the Illinois Central Railroad.

CHAPTER TWO
THE AMERICAN CIVIL WAR & WESTWARD EXPANSION
(1861–1875)

OPPOSITE
*A train travelling through
the Lackawanna Valley, as
painted by George Inness.*

By this time, however, Washington was the nominal capital of a nation at war, or in fact the capital of one of the two sides involved in the American Civil War. The expansion of the railroads was one of the factors that created the situation that did not so much lead to the start of the Civil War, but conditioned the ways in which the sides divided and the manner in which the war would be fought. The railroads had already created an essentially inter-related economic whole among the northern states, while the relative lack of similarly large railroad networks had contributed to the strong feeling of the rights of the southern states, individually as well as collectively, to decide their own futures. Although it was states' rights that were the root cause of the Civil War, the factor that brought this to the fore was slavery. Slavery had been permitted when Arkansas became a state in 1836, largely as a result of the Missouri Compromise of 1820, which allowed slavery in the region, but only on condition that it would not be permitted in the remaining lands west and north of the Arkansas border. During the 1850s the frontier steadily shifted to the west and more and more people poured into the area in their search for land, which made it essential that a new wave of organization should be implemented. This had major implications for the routes that the transcontinental railroads would use.

One of the first to appreciate this fact was Stephen Douglas, who saw that a single territory west of the Mississippi river would see its first settlers as people from Arkansas and Missouri who would without doubt create their main city in the south of the area, leading to a southward shift of the proposed railroad's course. Douglas wanted Chicago as the eastern end of the transcontinental railroad, so he planned a division of the area into two, with the question of slavery to be left to the people who reached the area: in this way Douglas hoped to make the area attractive to migrants from the north and the south. The result of this process was an 1854 act repealing the Missouri Compromise and establishing the new Kansas and Nebraska territories, but this act did not have the effect anticipated by Douglas. The northern opponents and southern proponents of slavery were respectively angered and pleased by the repeal of the Missouri Compromise, and in Kansas there developed an increasingly bitter and bloody war between the two sides. This bitterness was reflected in the 1860 presidential elections, in which the success of Abraham Lincoln and the Republican party led to the secession of the southern states, led by South Carolina, from the Union and then the outbreak of the Civil War between the Union and the Confederacy in the spring of 1861.

In simple terms, the dividing line between the two sides extended along the northern borders of Virginia, Tennessee and Arkansas. In the north lay more than two-thirds of the 31,000 miles (49890km) of U.S. railroads, which also constituted a

more useful concentration of transport capability than the more fragmented railroad network available to the Confederacy as a result of the more disjointed process of railroad development that had taken place in the southern states. Both sides were equally dependent on the portion of the complete American railroad system that lay in the areas they controlled, and to a very great extent the nature and extent of the railroad system was responsible for the way that the war between the states developed. It can sensibly be argued that it was only the availability of railroad transport that allowed the war to be fought in the way that it was, for the increasingly large armies mustered by each side were to a great extent reliant on the railroads, not only for strategic transport but also for the very considerable quantities of food, clothing, equipment and munitions that had to be delivered over considerable distances.

This fact was obvious from the start of the Civil War, and as a result, railroads became targets for raids from the beginning of hostilities. For example, the Baltimore & Ohio Railroad's bridge at Harpers Ferry had been destroyed by John Brown's raid on the town in 1859 and had then been reconstructed, only to be attacked by Stonewall Jackson in 1861 and destroyed once more. Jackson also commanded a raid on Martinsburg, when the Confederate attackers destroyed some 44 of the Baltimore & Ohio Railroad's locomotives. The Baltimore & Ohio line

The Pathfinders
Early Engineers in
the Cheat River Valley

was also frequently sabotaged by the Confederates, while farther to the south, the Norfolk & Petersburg and the South Side Railroads suffered major damage as battles were fought along their length. In many other areas of the railroad network, raiders attacked rolling stock and installations, burned bridges, cut telegraph lines and destroyed tracks within the context of both Union and Confederate efforts to disrupt their enemy's physical communications.

As the Civil War progressed, railroad transport became increasingly important for the movement of troops, together with all their equipment and munitions, for strategic and even tactical purposes. This tendency was evident from a very early stage, for in the war's first major battle, fought in July 1861 and known as the 1st Battle of Manassas by the Confederacy and the 1st Battle of Bull Run by the Union, victory went to the Confederacy as a result of the arrival by railroad of reinforcements at just the right moment. As the war proceeded, though, it was inevitable that the Union was in the better position to exploit its advantages in railroad transport capability. As noted above, the Confederacy was hindered by the comparatively small size and fragmented nature of the railroad network it inherited from the period before the war's outbreak: evidence of this fact can be found in July 1862, when General Braxton Bragg was able to move his army of 35,000 men from Tupelo in Mississippi to Chattanooga in Tennessee, but only via

Mobile on the Gulf of Mexico coast of Alabama in a loop that lengthened the journey by a factor of almost three.

Right through the war, the inherited deficiencies of the Confederacy's railroad system were compounded by the south's lack of industrial resources. Production of all the hardware associated with railroad operations, from rails to locomotives and the rolling stock they hauled, was concentrated in the northern states to the virtually total exclusion of the south, in which the continued rivalry between several of the railroad operators often caused the Confederacy's army enormous logistical problems.

It should not be inferred from this that the Union's railroad network was perfect, and operated by an organizational system that ran with complete smoothness. Certainly the Union's railroad system was wider-ranged, better integrated and possessed of generally superior equipment, but it also comprised tracks of several different gauges among a number of limitations. What the Union did achieve, though, was the maximization of the use it could extract from its railroad network. It was only in 1865, on the verge of its final defeat, that the Confederacy brought its railroad network totally under military control, but on the Union side it was 1862 when Lincoln received Congressional authorization to take over any railroad he considered necessary to the war effort. Perhaps even more important was the creation of the U.S. Military Railroads organization controlled

directly by the Department of War. Led by Daniel C. McCallum, the U.S. Military Railroads created just under 650 miles (1045km) of new track during the course of the war, and was also responsible for the construction of large numbers of bridges, finally controlling more than 2,000 miles (3220km) of track as well as more than 400 locomotives and 600 cars.

From a time in the middle of the war, the Union command had become sufficiently skilled in the effective use of the railroad system available to it that it had exploited this capability for the rapid movement of large numbers of troops. In September 1863, for example, Braxton Bragg's victory in the Battle of Chickamauga led to the investment of Chattanooga, where more than 20,000 Union soldiers (and vast quantities of materiel) were trapped under the command of General William Rosecrans. The Union command was then able, over a period of 12 days, to move two corps of the Army of the Potomac under the command of General Joseph Hooker some 1,190 miles (1915km) from defensive positions near Washington, D.C., to Bridgeport, one of the two points from which the relief of Chattanooga was then effected.

Naturally enough, the realization of the importance that effective use of railroad transport could have on the conduct of war went hand-in-hand with the perception that denial of this facility was equally significant. As a result, there were increasing efforts by each side

The Union locomotive Fred Leach, *after escaping from the Confederates. The holes in the smokestack show where the shots struck while she was working on the Orange & Alexandria Railroad near Inion Mills. 1st August 1863.*

during the Civil War to hamper if not actually deny the other side's use of the railroad system, generally by means of raids and sabotage as noted above. This meant that a comparatively small but nonetheless important proportion of each combatant's overall strength had to be deployed away from the front line for the protection of the railroads constituting the front line's primary lines of communication. One of the first to grasp the full implications of this concept was General William Sherman, one of the ablest commanders produced by the Union, in the course of his 1864 campaign. Sherman first built up his supplies at Nashville and Chattanooga in Tennessee, and then pushed back the Confederate forces along the line of the railroad toward Atlanta in Georgia, in the process severing the Confederacy's railroad links from Atlanta to Macon and Montgomery. This forced the Confederates to pull their Army of Tennessee, commanded by General Joseph Johnston and later General John Hood, south-east toward Atlanta. Sherman ensured that the railroad, crippled by the retreating Confederates, was repaired as he moved forward to allow the delivery of an unhindered supply of reinforcements, equipment and food. However, once he had arrived to the north-west of Atlanta and taken this key Confederate city under siege, Sherman found that he had to use about half of his available strength to protect the railroad.

This was one of the reasons for Sherman's classic change of tactics. Toward the end of the year Sherman decided to abandon the railroad and the assured delivery of supplies, instead striking off to the south-east in the great March to the Sea. Lasting from 15 November to 21 December, this took Sherman's forces in a wide swathe to Savannah in Georgia, and in the process divided the Confederacy into two portions that could then be defeated in detail. During the March to the Sea, Sherman's veteran forces lived off the land.

The Civil War ended in April 1865, and by this time the railroad network of the southern states was a shattered wreck over many of its most important sections. Even those sections that had not been destroyed were in a very poor state as a result of years of neglect and the absence of operational equipment. On the other side of what had been the front line, the situation was altogether different, for the years of the Civil War had seen extensive development of the northern states' railroad system. There had been considerable standardization of gauges, the tracks were in generally superior condition as steel had started to replace iron as the structural medium, and strides had been made toward the replacement of wood by coal as the primary fuel for locomotives. Most significant of all, though, was the new thinking that had swept into all matters pertaining to the creation and operation

Depot of the U.S. Military Railroads at City Point, Virginia, showing the engine President *in the foreground. 1864.*

The General Lowell, *an American-type 4-4-0 locomotive, photographed at Burlington, Iowa during the late Civil War period. The engine was named for Brigadier-General Charles Russell Lowell, Jnr., killed at the battle of Cedar Creek on 19 October 1864. Lowell had been assistant treasurer and land agent of the fledgling Burlington & Missouri River Railroad from its earliest days until he resigned on 25 October 1860 to become an ironmaker at Mt. Savage, Maryland. He was replaced by his assistant, 19-year-old Charles E. Perkins, who later became president of the Chicago, Burlington & Quincy Railroad.*

Engine No. 133 of the U.S. Military Railroads at City Point, Virginia. Built by Danforth, Cooke & Co., 1864.

of railroads. This was reflected in a revised attitude to the question of a transcontinental railroad link.

Agitation for the establishment of this link had continued unabated in Washington virtually throughout the Civil War. Its creation was seen from the outbreak of war in 1861 as something of national rather than merely financial significance: the establishment of closer physical links within the U.S.A. was clearly a factor that would deter further secessionist ambitions, perhaps by the states of the south-west and west, and the possibility of any southern route was clearly out of the question as all of these were based at their eastern ends in cities of the Confederacy. A starting point in Missouri was out of the question as there was major fighting in this region, resulting in the destruction of much of the railroad system already established there.

In the circumstances, therefore, it was little more than a formality when the relevant act was signed by Lincoln on 1 July 1862, which laid the legal framework for the construction of a railroad and parallel telegraph line from the Missouri river to the Pacific Ocean, and specified a starting point on the western side of Iowa's border. The new link was to be built simultaneously from the west and the east respectively by the Central Pacific Railroad and the newly-created Union Pacific Railroad.

The Congress imposed many conditions for the construction of the railroad to the Pacific: the builders were required to lay a single-track railroad and a telegraph line; the border between California and Nevada was to be fixed as the dividing line between the two companies' operations, the Central Pacific Railroad being allocated the area west of this line and the Union Pacific the area to the east of it; for land, the companies were each given a right of way 400ft (122m) in width as well as five alternating sections of land on each side for every mile of track completed. As far as financial resources were concerned, the two companies were allocated a $16,000 loan for each mile of track, rising to $32,000 and $48,000 per mile in foothill and mountain sections respectively. Both companies used their creative capabilities to maximize the theoretical distance of foothill and mountain they would have to traverse, which yielded the Union Pacific

A 2-6-0 locomotive on track repair work in the late 1860s.

Railroad $27 million and the Central Pacific $24 million, granted as first mortgages on the railroads. The railroad companies were also permitted to offer 100,000 $100 shares to the public, although no one person was allowed to purchase more than 200 shares, and no work was authorized until one-fifth of the shares had been bought. In order to benefit from these terms, the Union Pacific Railroad was required to complete 100 miles (160km) of track within two years and 100 miles per year thereafter.

The equivalent figures for the Central Pacific Railroad, working in more difficult terrain, were half of those demanded of the Union Pacific Railroad. Another official demand was that only American-produced iron was to be used.

At the same time, and in order to extend the benefits of the new railroad connection to areas in the same general vicinity as the eastern section of the new railroad link, permission was granted for the construction of lines east of 100° W to connect the new railroad link with cities

such as Omaha, Leavenworth, St. Joseph, Kansas City and Sioux City.

While Huntington was securing the charter to build the Central Pacific Railroad, Leland Stanford was elected governor of California and the Central Pacific Railroad received a state loan of $1.659 million. More money was found by selling bonds to the communities along the route, such as the sum of $1 million subscribed by San Francisco. There were fears that inland cities which did not subscribe would be bypassed by the new railroad and fade into commercial obscurity, and among the first of such subscribers was Sacramento and Placer County, which bought bonds to the total of $848,000.

On 8 January 1863, even as the Civil War was raging well to the east, Stanford broke the first ground for the Central Pacific Railroad's programme on the eastern bank of the Sacramento river. Another key player in the Central Pacific's leadership was Charles Crocker, who during this early phase of the programme had been working industriously to stockpile the required hardware at Sacramento. With the construction effort under way, Crocker became head of construction as general superintendent, and within six months 18 miles (29km) of track had been graded in preparation for the laying of the rails, and a 400-ft (122-m) trestle bridge had been built to cross the American river, which was, of course, only the first of very many major obstacles to the railroad's eastward

OPPOSITE
Hanover Junction (now Seven Valleys), Pennsylvania, at the time of the U.S. Civil War. The tall figure in the centre is thought to be President Lincoln. 1864.

LEFT
A key element of the Union forces' overall advantage over those of the Confederates in the Civil War was the larger and better organized system of railroads over which they were supplied, supported and reinforced. As they struck through the Confederate lines, as revealed in this photograph of part of General William T. Sherman's advance in 1864, the Union forces were generally at pains to rupture the Confederates' surviving railroad network.

BELOW LEFT
U.S. Military Railroads engine No. 137, built in the yards at Chattanooga, Tennessee, with troops lined up in the background. 1864.

RIGHT
What President Lincoln called the 'Beanpole & Cornstalk Bridge' over the Potomac Creek on the Richmond, Fredericksburg & Potomac Railroad.

BELOW
The American Civil War: picking up the debris of a derailed train after the retreat of John Pope's army at 2nd Bull Run, Virginia in 1863.

OPPOSITE
Ruins of the Confederate engine house at Atlanta, Georgia, showing engines Telegraph *and* O.A. Bull. *September 1864.*

advance. For the first 20 miles (32km) to Roseville, the climb from the altitude of Sacramento, which is only slightly above sea level, was very small, but from Roseville onward the construction crews were faced with ever-steeper gradients and, as the altitude rose, worse weather conditions.

One of the effort's main needs was large numbers of men to hack out rock and remove it, level the roadbed, and lay the ties and rails. Bridges up to 500ft (152m) in length and 100ft (30.5m) in height had to be extended across a large number of deep ravines that obstructed the route, tunnels 500 yards (457m) in length or more had to be driven through the hard stone ridges. Yet the Central Pacific Railroad could offer something in the order of only $2 or $3 per day for this work, which was demanding and at times very dangerous, at a time when the gold and silver mines of California offered the attractions of far higher wages. Crocker found a solution to the problem in the Chinese enclave of San Francisco, from which an initial 50 labourers were recruited. These soon revealed that they

RIGHT
The locomotive Thunder *with a passenger train on the Chicago & North Western Railroad near Rockford in the 1880s.*

OPPOSITE
The General *under steam on the Louisville & Nashville Railroad at Spurlington, Kentucky. Originally a wood burner, she later used diesel oil to heat the boiler. The coach is a 1913 model.*

The paymaster's car at Blue Creek station on the Union Pacific Railroad. From 250 in 1865, the construction crews grew to 10,000 by the time of the completion of the transcontinental railroad in 1869. About one in four were tracklayers, the remainder being graders, teamsters, herdsmen, cooks, bakers, blacksmiths, bridge-builders, carpenters, masons and clerks. On average they made $3 a day.

Central Pacific's roundhouse at Truckee in the Sierra Nevada Mountains, California, 1875.

could handle the work, and a large-scale programme of Chinese recruitment was launched: soon all the Chinese labour available in California had been drawn into the Central Pacific Railroad's workforce, and the railroad then had to find its manpower in China itself and then ship large numbers across the Pacific. By the summer of 1865 the Central Pacific Railroad's labourers totalled 4,000, of which some 3,500 or more were Chinese, and the railroad planned to double that number.

The Central Pacific Railroad also launched an imaginative scheme to support its financial planning and boost income. The directors of the Central Pacific created the Contract and Finance Corporation, to which the Central Pacific subcontracted the construction of the railroad. The Central Pacific Railroad

RIGHT

A construction train from General Casement's outfit near the railhead at Bear River City. Such trains included flatcars for tools, a forge for blacksmithing, coaches for sleeping in and other cars for cooking, eating and storage. 1868.

OPPOSITE

The locomotive John G. Read, *named for a Burlington & Missouri River Railroad vice-president. The photograph was taken at Burlington, Iowa. The locomotive was built by Manchester in 1866.*

RIGHT
Advertisement for the Chicago & North Western Railroad's Short Line.

FAR RIGHT
The Baltimore & Ohio Railroad's station at Camden. 1869.

Snowsheds and Chinese labourers on the Central Pacific Railroad. The painting is by Joseph Becker, 1869.

RIGHT

Atchison, Topeka & Santa Fe's locomotive No. 5, Thomas Sherlock, *built in 1870 by the Taunton Locomotive Company and scrapped in 1911 after 41 years of service.*

OPPOSITE

Harrisburg, Pennsylvania. The station in the 1860s, just after the Civil War. Shown here are trains operated by four railroads, the Pennsylvania, Northern Central, Cumberland Valley, and the Philadelphia & Reading. The first three are now included in the Pennsylvania Railroad system.

A train at City Point, Virginia, awaiting to transport troops to the front during the Civil War in 1864.

A train on the U.S. Military Railroads, crossing a guarded bridge on the Orange &Alexandria Railroad during the Civil War.

RIGHT

Excavating for a 'Y' at Devereux station on the Orange & Alexandria Railroad. Brigadier-General Hermann Haupt, chief of Construction & Transportation, U.S. Military Railroads, is standing on the bank supervising the work. The locomotive General Haupt *heads the work train.*

OPPOSITE

Central Pacific Railroad's locomotive Jupiter *with bandsmen from the 21st Infantry, stationed at Fort Douglas, Utah, at the completion of the transcontinental railway at Promontory Point, Utah on 10 May 1869.*

eventually paid the Contract and Finance Corporation almost $80 million, a figure about twice as large as it should have been. Thus vast quantities of federal and shareholder money passed from one to the other. In 1866 Congress authorized the Central Pacific Railroad to continue to the east of the state line that it had originally fixed as its eastern limit.

The increase in the labour force and the imaginative use of its financial resources allowed the Central Pacific Railroad to speed its progress to the east. During June 1864, it issued its first timetable, a schedule for the 31 miles (50km) of track between Sacramento and Newcastle: three trains per day, one of them carrying passengers and mail and the other two loaded with passengers and

freight, were interspersed with trains carrying labourers and materials to the railhead. The next 12 miles (19.3km), climbing 800ft (244m) to Clipper Gap, took 12 months, but in the following two months 11-miles (17.7-km) more were added to the length of the operator's tracks. Grading of the trackway continued through the winter, and by the end of 1866 the track had reached Cisco, only 92 miles (148km) from Sacramento, but at an altitude of almost 6,000ft (1829m).

The next winter was horrendous: in February and March the snow averaged more than 10ft (3m) in depth, blizzards battered the work camps for days on end, and the cold was intense. Even so, work on the track continued, for the Central

The American Civil War & Westward Expansion (1861–1875)

Pacific Railroad could not afford to pay men who were not working, or to lose a workforce which was now very skilled in its multitudinous tasks. As a great snow plough was used to keep open the track back to Sacramento and snowsheds were built to protect the track behind and the newly graded roadbed ahead, the labourers began work on the 1,659-ft (506-m) Summit Tunnel at an altitude of 7,108ft (2139m): 8,000 men hacked and blasted their way from each end and also in both directions from a central shaft, and after the compacted snow had prevented even a team of 12 locomotives from moving the snow plough, oxen were employed to deliver the quantities of timber, explosives and supplies that were needed by the labour force.

Next, the men of the Central Pacific Railroad reached the Donner Pass, and here in 1867 the last snow did not disappear until June. The melting snow finally allowed the ties and rails to be laid on the new roadbed, and by mid-1867 the Central Pacific Railroad had advanced some 130 miles (209km) from its western end; however, the rails though the Summit Tunnel were not to be laid until the end of the year. Three locomotives hauled 40 cars to the summit, and then there followed all the resources for another 50 miles (80km) of track, teams of oxen being used to overcome the gap in the rails. Even so, weather conditions militated against major progress by the Central Pacific Railroad in 1867, when it completed the laying of only another 40

miles (64km) of track that reached the border between California and Nevada in December; there was a gap of 7 miles (11.25km) near Donner Lake, where work had been halted by snow. The rails reached the new city of Reno in Nevada during the spring of 1868, the gap in the rails near Donner Lake was filled and, with equipment and supplies now brought up more easily, the railhead was advanced across Nevada toward Utah. The Central Pacific Railroad was now beginning to reap the benefits of completed track, with traffic to and from the rich mining area of Nevada boosting income quite dramatically; the board of directors now wanted to reach Ogden before the westward advance of the Union Pacific Railroad claimed it.

The Union Pacific Railroad had been slower off the mark, starting with the receipt of its charter by an 1862 act of the Congress that named 158 commissioners. Some of these conducted a preliminary meeting in Chicago during September 1862, when William B. Ogden was elected as president. Thomas Durant, the man behind the Rock Island Railroad and its subsidiary, the Mississippi & Missouri Railroad, wanted another man, however, and set about overturning this initial decision. In March 1863, with only 150 shares on the Union Pacific Railroad sold, Durant used the names of friends to bypass the provisions governing share ownership and, by selling his holding in the Mississippi & Missouri Railroad, secured control of the 20,000 shares that

had to be sold before work could begin. In October 1863, therefore, Durant was able to use the major shareholding he controlled to oust Ogden in favour of John A. Dix, previously the figurehead president of the Mississippi & Missouri Railroad.

Only a short time later, on 2 December of the same year, ground was broken at the start of the Union Pacific Railroad's eastern end at Omaha. But by spring of the next year, the Union Pacific Railroad had completed only a few miles of initial grading and work had halted for the lack of adequate funding at a critical time in the Civil War. Durant's solution was the establishment of the Credit Mobilier of America as a holding company, and the persuasion of the Congress to double the Union Pacific Railroad's land grant and to include with it any mineral deposits under the land, to convert the company's federal loans into a second mortgage, and increase the permitted number of shares from 100,000 to one million. A final touch in Durant's plan was the replacement of Peter Dey, the chief engineer who had estimated costs at between $20,000 and $30,000 per mile, by Colonel Silas Seymour, who had prepared a more circuitous line of advance and the arrangement with the Credit Mobilier for work to be completed on the basis of $50,000 per mile.

These dealings were dubious in a number of respects, but did have the effect of bringing in more financial resources and thereby permitting work to

The Golden Spike ceremony at Promontory Point, Utah on 10 May 1869.

Commodore Cornelius Vanderbilt (1794–1877), U.S. financier and railroad baron.

be resumed on a practical basis. This was just as well for the Union Pacific Railroad, for already the Leavenworth, Pawnee & Western Railroad, in its new guise as the Union Pacific, Eastern Division, and with its own federal land grant agreed, was driving west from the Missouri river; the Atchison & Topeka Railroad under Cyrus K. Holliday had also received federal land grants encouraging it to revise its original thinking, based on the construction of a railroad from Atchison on the Missouri river to Topeka, the capital of Kansas, to ambitious plans for a westward extension along the Santa Fe Trail to the Pacific.

Events soon proved that Seymour was a poor choice to supervise the construction of the Union Pacific Railroad's line, for by October 1865 only 15 miles (24km) of track had been completed. Seymour was therefore replaced by General Grenville Dodge, who had been Peter Dey's assistant on the Rock Island Railroad, had been involved in the surveys for the Mississippi & Missouri Railroad, and had distinguished himself in the Civil War. At much the same time, in the spring of 1866, the company took on General John S. Casement and his brother Daniel to supervise construction. These changes soon began to transform the rate of progress. The ferry landing at Omaha on the western bank of the Missouri river developed into an industrial town as workshops sprang up, boats delivered masses of equipment and supplies, and a workforce of 10,000 men and large

The Golden Spike ceremony at Utah's Promontory Point to celebrate the joining of the Union Pacific and Central Pacific Railroads and the completion of the first trans-America link. 10 May 1869.

OPPOSITE
Section men turning out for work on the building of the Southern Pacific line in the mountains near the entrance to the San Fernando tunnel, just north of Los Angeles in 1875.

numbers of draft animals were assembled.

As the line advanced to the west, an accommodation train was built with triple-deck bunks, and other trains brought ties and rails closer to the railhead for final delivery by wagons hauled by horses. Still farther forward, the grading teams were supplied by trains of ox-hauled wagons, and right at the front of the whole process the route was surveyed and fixed by special parties. The reorganization of the whole process sped progress by a factor of up to seven, so that by October 1866 the Union Pacific Railroad's new line had crossed the line at 100° W, just under 250 miles (400km) to the west of Omaha, and just a few weeks later, winter quarters had been constructed at North Platte.

In the spring of 1867 the Chicago & North Western Railroad reached Council Bluffs, easing supply problems considerably, and at the same time the Union Pacific Railroad began work once more. By the onset of the winter of 1867–68, the new line had reached the newly-constructed camp at Cheyenne, now a community with a population of 4,000. The Union Pacific Railroad's line of advance now took it through the Black Hills at about the time that the Central Pacific Railroad was pushing forward into Nevada after passing over and through the mountain barrier that had proved so troublesome.

Both of the new railroads were now aiming to be first into Utah, and Dodge declared his intention of doubling the 500 miles (805km) already laid and reaching Ogden by the end of 1868. To further their aims, both the Union Pacific and Central Pacific Railroads placed contracts with the Mormons in Utah to begin grading routes far ahead of their rails, but an unfortunate aspect of this move was that many miles of parallel routing were graded before the federal authorities fixed on Ogden as the meeting place.

The tracklaying operation was now a finely tuned operation that was pushed ahead on a massive scale. Before work began in 1868, 3,000 men were busy cutting down trees and siting the trunks along the Union Pacific Railroad's path, and the work train was enlarged to accommodate butchers, bakers and even an occasional visitor such as a newspaper publisher. Hell on Wheels, was the name bestowed on the camp followers with their portable saloons, and this followed the railhead through Laramie, Benton, Red Desert, Black Butte, Green River, Salt Wells, and Bitter Creek in southern Wyoming.

Before the onset of winter slowed the construction season once more, the Union Pacific's railhead had reached Wasatch in the mountains of the border between Wyoming and Utah, a mere 67 miles (108km) from Ogden and 995 miles (1601km) to the west of Omaha. On the other side of the race, the Central Pacific Railroad had reached a point some 446 miles (718km) east of Sacramento at Carlin in the north-eastern part of Nevada. With Ogden so close, neither railroad was prepared to consider a winter break, even though conditions in the mountains were very bad. The pay of the labourers was doubled, work continued, and by the spring both railroads were racing across the plains of Utah. The Union Pacific Railroad was first to reach Ogden, on 8 March, and by this point barely 50 miles (80km) separated the two railheads. Even so, it was only because of pressure exerted by President Ulysses S. Grant that the two railroads finally agreed on a meeting place, namely Promontory some 53 miles (85km) west of Ogden.

By now the telegraph line paralleling the tracks had been completed, and on a daily basis newspaper reports of the rival organizations' progress were gripping the country. Crocker and the Casements responded by doubling and redoubling the daily mileage until each railhead was advancing between 6 and 8 miles (9.7 and 12.9km) each day. The rivalry between the Central Pacific Railroad's Chinese and the Union Pacific's generally Irish workforces became more than merely intense, and there were instances of work gangs deliberately setting off explosive charges round each other's positions.

The culmination of the transcontinental railroad construction effort arrived on 28 April. With only some 20 miles (32km) of track still to be laid, Crocker decided a $10,000 bet he had made with Durant by having a specially selected team lay 10 miles (16km) of rail in only 12 hours.

It was all over in just a few more days. On 10 May 1869 officers and workers of the two railroads gathered at Promontory for the placing of a silver-wreathed laurel tie and the driving of a golden spike to mark the junction of the rails. The Union Pacific Railroad's locomotive, *Jupiter*, and the Central Pacific Railroad's No. 119 crept forward to touch each other, alcohol flowed, and a telegraph message signalled the completion of the first trans-continental railroad.

The celebrations of this great achievement swept the U.S.A.: a 100-gun salute in New York was echoed by the ringing of the Liberty Bell in Philadelphia, and there was a huge procession in Chicago. But the celebrations were to be succeeded by bitterness and a sad day of reckoning that would gravely disturb all Americans. The overall cost of the first transcontinental railroad was truly enormous. The Union Pacific Railroad had collected land grants totalling 24 million acres (9600000 hectares) and the Central Pacific Railroad 9 million acres (3600000 hectares) for a combined total of more than 50,000 square miles (130000km²). Government grants to the two companies amounted to $27 million and $24 million respectively, quite apart from the further huge sums raised from the sale of stock. In 1869, few doubted that this was money well spent. Even the fact that the rail lines, especially that of the Union Pacific Railroad, were poor in quality was at first overlooked in the heat of the overall achievement. Other factors that could be

ignored in the excitement of the moment or explained by the speed with which the two railroads had pushed forward their work were randomly spaced ties placed unballasted on the ground; the use of soft unseasoned pine for ties that started to rot as they were laid; poorly built bridges; unshored embankments; poor joining of rail; and a deliberately meandering route, clearly chosen to maximize land grants. The general feeling was that the important factor was that rail

communications across the country were now possible, and that time would see the improvement of the track and the straightening of the route.

It was in 1873 that the real shock arrived, for it was in this year that it was revealed that numbers of Congressmen had received stock in the Credit Mobilier, which had been able to pay huge dividends on the basis of its fraudulent dealings with the Union Pacific Railroad. The Credit Mobilier scandal caused a

national outrage that quickly eroded the public's faith in the railroads. An immediate consequence of this was a disastrous fall in the value of the Union Pacific Railroad's shares: by the end of 1873 they had dropped from $100 to $14, a fact that caught the attention of Jay Gould. Gould had established himself as a hard-headed businessman in his battles with Cornelius Vanderbilt over the New York railroads.

The growth of the railroads across the U.S.A. was a matter not only of the laying of track and the manufacture of locomotives and rolling stock, but also of creating the logistical infrastructure required for the effective and therefore economic operation of the growing railroad system. This meant the creation and maintenance of fuel stockpiles and, as seen here, the erection of water towers at the right intervals.

CHAPTER THREE
CONSOLIDATION AND THE
RAILROAD BARONS (1875–1917)

Virtually the only large industrial concerns before the Civil War, railroads had been popular with speculators in stocks and shares since the 1830s. During the Civil War, Vanderbilt and others had made large sums from speculation in railroad shares, and by the end of the war Vanderbilt had used his holdings in the Harlem Railroad to force the directors of the New York Central Railroad, which was reliant on the Harlem Railroad for its New York connection, to surrender control of the operation to him. At the same time, two younger adventurers, Jay Gould and Jim Fisk, had managed to take control of the Erie system from Daniel Drew, one of the first railroad speculators, who had taken over the Erie in the 1850s solely to facilitate speculation in its shares. Vanderbilt's New York Central system was at least soundly organized and well run, while the Erie system was notable for its neglected condition and high accident rate, since virtually none of the operation's resources

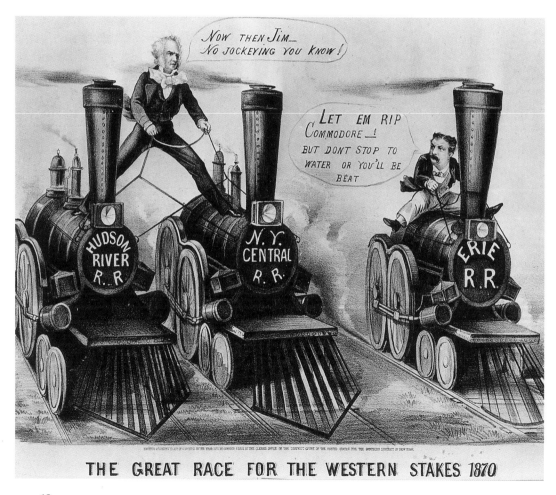

THE GREAT RACE FOR THE WESTERN STAKES 1870

An Illinois Central Railroad poster by Swaim & Lewis. 1882.

were spent on track and rolling stock.

Gould and Fisk further enlarged Drew's type of manipulation of the Erie, and in the late 1860s their battles with Vanderbilt reached an extraordinary level. Early in 1868, for example, they were forced to flee New York to avoid arrest, and then established their headquarters in Jersey City. Later, after a series of legal and political conflicts in which judges and

state legislators were liberally bribed (often by each side), Fisk and Gould were able to return to New York, where they based themselves in a vaudeville theatre with a basement in which a printing press produced a constant stream of Erie stock certificates.

The Erie battle ended in compromise, and Gould turned his sights on farther targets. He began with speculation in the

Wabash and Lake Shore lines along the southern shores of the Great Lakes, then concentrated his efforts to corner the U.S.A.'s entire gold supply as a step toward a reduction in the export price of grain and thus the stimulation of traffic on the grain-carrying Wabash: this scheme was prevented by the intervention of the authorities, but Gould managed to sell just in time; after the Credit Mobilier scandal

OPPOSITE
Members of a Northern Pacific Railroad construction crew pose with their work train at a bridge crossing Green river in the Cascade range of Washington Territory. These men were part of forces committed to building North Pacific's famed switchback route over these mountains in 1886. The route was used just prior to and during construction of the Stampede Tunnel. The latter was completed in May 1888.

LEFT
A Northern Pacific passenger train at Taylor Falls, Minnesota in the 1880s.

OPPOSITE

A Baldwin 2-8-2 engine of California & Western Railroad at Fort Bragg, California.

LEFT

St. Paul, Minneapolis & Manitoba locomotive No. 158. Built in August 1882, it was retired in November 1918.

he began buying up the low-cost stock of the Union Pacific Railroad. As had been the case with his Erie operation, Gould saw this as an exercise in pure speculation, and controlled the Union Pacific Railroad only as long as it took to make enormous sums for himself by declaring unjustifiably high dividends before he sold his holdings at the inflated prices this produced. In 1878 he turned to the bankrupt Kansas Pacific Railroad and, after settling with the bondholders, announced his plan to construct a line from Denver to the west coast. By this measure he forced the new board of the Union Pacific Railroad to take over the Kansas Pacific Railroad to protect their monopoly of the route: once again, the price of his holdings soared, and

Gould again sold at an enormous profit.

Quite different from that of Gould, the financial control of Huntington interests was both orthodox and sound. Huntington's thinking extended beyond Durant's concept of exploiting just one railroad, and while he was as interested as Gould in increasing his wealth, Huntington achieved this aim in a businesslike rather than purely speculative fashion as he wanted to hold on to the businesses he created. In addition to enlarging his interests to include west coast shipping and other related industries, Huntington was moving in the direction of a second independent transcontinental railroad even before the two sections of the first

had been connected at Promontory.

In 1868, Huntington and his group of investors bought the charter for the Southern Pacific Railroad as a first step in consolidating their position in California. The Contract and Finance Company, having absorbed some $79 million for its part in the construction of the Central Pacific Railroad, was replaced by the Western Development Company, which was established to further the group's exploitation of the fertile but currently underpopulated state.

The new organization's first step was the creation of a railroad through the San Joaquin valley from San Francisco to Los Angeles, and with the help of generous grants from Los Angeles the new line was completed by 1876. The next step was to fight off others who were interested in building a southern railroad to the west coast. The most important of these was the Texas & Pacific Railroad, which had been chartered with a federal land grant of some 18 million acres (7200000 hectares) along the Mexican border. The Texas & Pacific Railroad was headed by Thomas A. Scott, president of the leading eastern operator, the Pennsylvania Railroad. Scott had previously tried to run the Union Pacific Railroad but had soon abandoned the idea and now employed Grenville Dodge to build the new railroad. In 1873 there were problems as Dodge was implicated in the Credit Mobilier scandal and the inward flow of funds ceased. The Texas & Pacific Railroad reached Dallas in 1873, but by 1876 it had progressed only

OPPOSITE
*This beautifully preserved
and restored 4-6-0
locomotive, No. 200, is seen
in the colours of the Texas
State Railroad.*

LEFT
*The first passenger train into
Minnewaukon, 10 August
1885.*

as far as Fort Worth, less than 200 miles (322km) from its starting point at Marshall.

In 1877 Scott, Huntington and the federal authorities reached an agreement by which the Southern Pacific Railroad would retain control of the California end of the new transcontinental route and that Scott would extend the Texas & Pacific Railroad to Yuma on the border between Arizona and California and provide connection to the east.

Having extended the Southern Pacific Railroad as far as Yuma, Huntington was fixed on the idea of further development and secured charters from the territorial governments of Arizona and New Mexico to circumvent the lack of federal backing. Bridging the Colorado river and presenting the government with a *fait accompli*, he won presidential approval for his plan to continue building eastward. The competing railroads finally fixed a junction at El Paso on the border between

New Mexico and Texas, where the two lines met in 1882 to complete a second transcontinental railroad. In 1883 the Southern Pacific Railroad acquired its own route across Texas by taking over the Galveston, Harrisburg & San Antonio Railroad which, along with other small lines, eventually gave the Southern Pacific Railroad a route to New Orleans, and finally in 1895 the Central Pacific Railroad was absorbed into the new system.

This is only one part of the unfolding

Union Pacific's locomotive No. 574 (4-4-0) heading a passenger train at Genoa, Nebraska. The engineer is H.A. Riley, fireman E.P. Rogers, conductor Harry Schaffer and brakeman W.F. McFadden. 1894.

This picture, taken at Rocklin, California in 1890, shows Central Pacific locomotive No. 82, built by Rogers in 1868. The cordwood piled in the tender is ready for use as fuel. Four-wheel 15-ft (4.5-m) 'dinky' cabooses, like the one shown in this photograph, were in operation on the Central Pacific and Southern Lines.

story of railroad construction toward the Pacific, for during this period there were other railroads driving through the south-western states of the U.S.A. The Denver & Rio Grande Railroad was established by the citizens of the state capital to boost the development of the new mines in the Rocky Mountains in Colorado. The Kansas Pacific Railroad had been built between Denver and Kansas City, and was linked to the Union Pacific Railroad at Cheyenne by a northward branch. The new line was directed south toward Santa Fe, also the objective of another ambitious programme, in this instance by the Atchison, Topeka & Santa Fe Railroad.

Since receiving its Kansas land grant in 1863, the Atchison, Topeka & Santa Fe

Railroad made only the most limited progress until 1870, when it began building across Kansas on the commercial basis of the burgeoning cattle trade centred on Dodge City, a city the line reached during 1872. A year later the railroad reached La Junta in the south-east of Colorado, and at much the same time the Denver & Rio Grande Railroad reached Pueblo, 70 miles (113km) farther to the west. Both lines were then checked by the financial problems following the Credit Mobilier scandal, but by 1876 the Topeka & Santa Fe Railroad had also reached Pueblo.

Up to this time the fights between the western railroads had been financial and political, but now they escalated in armed

CYRUS K. HOLLIDAY
1826 – 1900
PIONEER AND BUILDER
FOUNDER AND MAYOR OF TOPEKA.
INFLUENCED THE SELECTION OF THIS CITY
AS THE CAPITAL OF KANSAS.
ORGANIZED THE ATCHISON, TOPEKA AND
SANTA FE RAILROAD COMPANY. OBTAINED
THE ORIGINAL CHARTER IN THE YEAR 1859.
PROMOTED THE EARLY DEVELOPMENT OF
KANSAS AND THE ENTIRE SOUTHWEST.

OPPOSITE,
LEFT
Memorial plaque to Cyrus K. Holliday, incorporator and first president of the Atchison, Topeka & Santa Fe Railroad.

RIGHT
A photograph of Cyrus K Holliday.

LEFT
Lady travellers enjoy some extemporary music aboard a Santa Fe Railroad Pullman in the early 1900s.

Union Pacific locomotive No. 934 heads a block fruit train (before refrigerated cars were developed) in Nebraska or West Wyoming. Circa 1890.

battles. The only route south to Santa Fe lay through the Raton Pass on the New Mexico border, while the other objective of the rival railroads, namely the mining area around Leadville to the west of Pueblo, could be reached only through the Royal Gorge of the Arkansas river. With the approval of the toll road operator through the Raton Pass, the construction teams of the Atchison, Topeka & Santa Fe Railroad arrived in February 1872 and prepared to start grading work. They were opposed by armed employees of the Denver & Rio Grande Railroad, but local feeling had

been turned against the latter by some extremely dubious real estate operations, and the Santa Fe men fought off their rivals to secure the route to the south. Further battles followed over the right of way through the Royal Gorge, but the matter was finally settled in the courts in favour of the Denver & Rio Grande Railroad.

The Atchison, Topeka & Santa Fe Railroad then decided to concentrate of areas farther to the west, and in pursuance of this object in 1880 bought the old charter for the Atlantic & Pacific Railroad,

planned as a connection between St. Louis and southern California but currently extending no farther than the border of Missouri. In the east, a line was built from the Atchison, Topeka & Santa Fe Railroad's tracks at Wichita to a junction with the Atlantic & Pacific Railroad at Pierce City, near Springfield in Missouri, giving the Atchison, Topeka & Santa Fe a link to the east at St. Louis. In the west, the charter of the Atlantic & Pacific Railroad included large land grants in Arizona and New Mexico, and this allowed the Atchison, Topeka & Santa Fe Railroad to

Part of Baltimore & Ohio's massive port facilities at Locust Point, Baltimore, Maryland. This view shows immigrants who had arrived at pier 8 or 9, and been processed in the immigrant centre (left), preparing to board trains for the West. 1880.

CONSOLIDATION AND THE RAILROAD BARONS (1875–1917)

BELOW
New York Central's
Twentieth Century
Limited. *1902.*

OPPOSITE
Atchison, Topeka & Santa Fe
Railroad locomotive No. 457,
a Class 454 4-6-0 type, built
in 1899 by the Dickson
Locomotive Works for
passenger service.

lay a new line to Albuquerque in New Mexico. This meant that the city of Santa Fe was now served only by a branch, while the main line carried on to the California border at Needles, one of the few places along the Colorado river that could be bridged using the technology of the day. The Southern Pacific Railroad had already built its own line to Needles, and an agreement between the two companies allowed the Atchison, Topeka & Santa Fe to operate its trains to Los Angeles and San Francisco, thereby creating a third transcontinental line.

Over the same period, another railroad to the Pacific coast was being created much farther to the north. This was the child of the Northern Pacific Railroad, and extended along the route from Lake Superior to Portland in Oregon that Asa Whitney had advocated as early as 1845. During the Civil War, when the Pacific railroad charters were created, the Northern Pacific Railroad had been granted 47 million acres (18800000 hectares) in the north-west region of the U.S.A. between Minnesota and Washington state, but there had been no direct financial subsidies to go with the land grants; this delayed the start of work by five years. In 1869 Jay Cooke, the Philadelphia financier who had created most of his wealth through the sale of the government bonds that financed the Union during the Civil War and had reinvested much of it in large tracts of land in Minnesota, entered the picture. After undertaking his own survey of the Northern Pacific Railroad's allocated route, Cooke became the railroad's financial agent. Cooke hired newspaper editors and public figures to extol the advantages of the north-western U.S.A., and so attractive did the region seem in the advertising material that the curved belt of land in the accompanying maps became generally known as Jay Cooke's Banana Belt. This publicity campaign aimed to sell $100 million of bonds in order to finance the building of the railroad.

It was in 1870 that work began, and soon branches from Duluth and Minneapolis met at Brainerd before extending westward across Minnesota and Dakota to the banks of the Missouri river, where in 1873 the new town of Bismarck was established. The naming of this city after the German chancellor was part of an attempt to gain both investment and

RIGHT

Henry Villard, president of the Northern Pacific Railroad in 1883, when the first transcontinental line was completed, linking Lake Superior with Puget Sound.

FAR RIGHT

James J. Hill in a touring car at Vancouver, Washington.

RIGHT

Henry Villard, president of the Northern Pacific Railroad in 1883, when the first transcontinental line was completed, linking Lake Superior with Puget Sound.

FAR RIGHT

James J. Hill in a touring car at Vancouver, Washington.

immigrants from Germany. The railroad had been spending rather more quickly than Cooke could raise money through the sale of bonds, however, and Cooke's bank was subsidizing the railroad to the tune of some $5.5 million. Cooke attempted to regain the advantage by the sale of a new issue of government bonds, but there was little market for these. The Credit Mobilier scandal and rumours of the Northern Pacific Railroad's difficulties, combined with a number of adverse reports concerning conditions along the Banana

Belt, now made it even trickier than before to sell new railroad bonds. Cooke's problems were compounded by the fact that the Franco-Prussian War had made the flow of European capital to North America slow to a trickle, and on 18 September 1873, the closure of the New York offices of Cooke's bank signalled the start of a major financial crash.

By this time, the railroads had received some $3 billion from the authorities and the public, and between 1865 and 1870 railroads in the U.S.A. had expanded from

35,000 to 53,000 miles (56325 to 85295km). This was impressive, but far less so was the state of the investment market that was supporting the railroads: in 1860 each mile of railroad was supported by an average of 1,026 investors, but by 1873 that figure had declined to just 590. The result was the collapse of the financial system and many of the railroads all over the U.S.A., though the Northern Pacific Railroad managed to avoid bankruptcy until 1875.

Money, or rather the lack of it, was

Missouri Pacific locomotive No. 6509, a Pacific-type 4-6-2, built in 1903 by the American Locomotive Company (Alco) for passenger services.

only one of the problems afflicting further development of the U.S. railroad network at this time. In the north-west, Native Americans, who had been forced to the north by the westward encroachment of the railroads into their hunting grounds, now refused to shift farther or allow more railroad construction. The military expedition to quell the disaffection of the Native Americans led to the defeat of Colonel George Custer's 7th Cavalry Regiment in the Battle of the Little Big Horn in 1876. After that final victory, Chief Sitting Bull led the tribes north into Canada and peace was re-established in the north-west, the financial situation improved, and once more there was a revival of interest in the creation of a northern transcontinental railroad link.

Henry Villard, a journalist and a

German by origin, had represented German bondholders in the bankruptcy of the Kansas Pacific Railroad and in the process gained a considerable reputation as a result of his fight for repayment of the debts. Villard now received a commission to look after the interests of a similar group which had invested in the bankrupt Oregon & California Railroad. Villard began by incorporating the Oregon Railway & Navigation Company, which rapidly become the most important transport factor in the area. Villard constructed railroads along the Columbia and Willamette river valleys, and this led to his notion of building his own transcontinental railroad. The Northern Pacific Railroad still controlled the land grants, however, and from 1875 was being revitalized by Frederick Billing; it began to

James Jerome Hill, U.S. financier and railroad executive, c. 1890.

RIGHT
Boston & Maine's American Standard locomotive No. 150 has just moved out of the engine house in Danvers, Massachusetts. Circa 1895.

LEFT
An early passenger train of the late 1880s or 1890s, probably taken between Great Falls and Butte on the line of the Montana Central Railway, which later became part of the Great Northern Railway.

RIGHT
Baltimore & Ohio Railroad's EL-2-class Mallet 2-8-8-0. 1916.

BELOW
L-class 4-8-0 Mastadon locomotive (No. 2909) outside the engine house at Rochester, New Hampshire. 1912.

LEFT

Northern Pacific wood-burning locomotives brought excitement to Missoula, Montana in 1883, when they arrived in a fleet to help power the first trains across the North-West. Tracks through Missoula were completed on 23 June 1883 by a construction crew, building eastwards from the Columbia river. This interesting photograph shows the typical engine houses of the day, later to give way to the roundhouses.

BELOW LEFT

Three 2-8-0 locomotives with a wedge snowplough and accommodation coach used on the Grand Rapids & Indiana. 1905.

push the line forward toward Tacoma in Washington state and the natural harbours of the Puget Sound rather than to Portland in Oregon, 100 miles (160km) inland.

Villard offered the Northern Pacific Railroad the use of his Columbia river valley tracks for its western end, but when the offer was turned down, Villard created a blind pool (money raised from a number of investors without disclosure of the purpose) and gained control of the Northern Pacific Railroad. But Villard was now beginning to get out of his own depth, and the cost of construction, especially over immensely difficult sections across the Rocky Mountains, climbed above the railroad's financial resources. By the end of the year, the Northern Pacific Railroad had gone into liquidation, Villard resigning and the railroad being reorganized financially to allow its completion to Tacoma.

Its huge land grants seemed to have given the Northern Pacific Railroad an unassailable monopoly on the northern route to the Pacific, but another great financier, James J. Hill, who had made his fortune in the grain trade of St. Paul in Minnesota, was another entrepreneur with his sights set on the region. His opportunity came in the form of yet another of the railroads bankrupted in the aftermath of the 1873 scandal and resulting panic. It was in 1862 that the St. Paul & Pacific Railroad had received its charter along with a land grant of 5 million acres (2000000 hectares) of Minnesota, but had advanced its line only

OPPOSITE & LEFT
Where water crossings were too long for the practical and safe construction of bridges, the railroads had to use specially designed and manufactured ferries. These had to be relatively wide, quite long, and as low to the water as possible. They also had to possess open decks outfitted with rails.

to a link-up with the Northern Pacific Railroad's operation at Brainerd and the creation of a branch line toward the Canadian border. In 1878 Hill succeeded in gaining control of the St. Paul & Pacific Railroad by buying its stock for a fraction of the face value, and then turned a healthy profit by selling the associated

land. Hill changed the name of the organization to the St. Paul, Minneapolis & Manitoba Railroad and began to drive the line forward in the direction of the Canadian border and a junction with the new Canadian Pacific Railway at Pembina.

The arrival of large numbers of immigrants in the northern part of

Minnesota and several years of very good grain crops combined to boost Hill's financial resources, allowing him to extend the railroad. Hill was decidedly dissimilar from the majority of speculative railroad operators before him, for he proceeded slowly and carefully, dictated efficient operations, and charged lower rates than

his primary competitor, the Northern Pacific Railroad, to increase the likelihood of a regular flow of income. During the 1880s the railhead moved slowly but steadily to the west through the timber and copper mining areas of Montana.

In January 1893 the Great Northern route to the Puget Sound at Seattle in Washington state was complete, and before the end of the year the Northern Pacific Railroad, whose control Villard had managed to regain during 1889, was bankrupt once more; by 1896 Hill had gained control of the route parallel to the one that he himself had built. Hill had a further ambition, however, and now desired to extend toward Chicago and the Midwest.

The possible means to this end were two in number. The Chicago, Burlington & Quincy Railroad had been created in

OPPOSITE
Buffalo bone pickers and Red River carts at the Northern Pacific Railroad yard at Minnewaukan, Dakota Territory, 24 May 1886.

LEFT
Large-scale hauling of wheat from ranches to Scobey, Montana in 1921, for shipment to markets over the Great Northern Railway.

BELOW LEFT
Baltimore & Ohio Railroad workshops at Piedmont (west of Keyser), West Virginia, at the foot of the '17-mile grade' from Piedmont to Altamont, Maryland, on the line to Wheeling and Parkersburg. Circa 1875.

1856 through the amalgamation of a couple of small lines in the Chicago area, and over the years it had developed though line extensions and takeovers into a system of over 6,000 miles (9655km), extending from Chicago to points as far removed as Denver, Kansas City, Minneapolis, St. Louis and points in Montana. The alternative was the Chicago, Milwaukee & St. Paul Railroad, but this had the backing of William Rockefeller, the creator of Standard Oil, and was not for sale, so Hill bought the Chicago, Burlington & Quincy Railroad.

It is worth noting that, by this time, the word transcontinental had lost much of its significance as far as the railroads and the public were concerned. There was no single line linking the Atlantic and the Pacific seaboards of the U.S.A., although one man who almost managed to create such an entity, about 10 years later, was George Gould. Until the panic of 1907, Gould had numbered the Denver & Rio Grande Western, the Wabash and the Western Maryland Railroads among his extensive railroad interests, and with the completion of his Western Pacific Railroad in 1909, linking Ogden and San Francisco, Gould came close to achieving a system that spanned the continent from sea to shining sea,.

But the creation of transcontinental links was not the only desire of railroad entrepreneurs in the western part of the U.S.A.; railroads were built wherever there was a perceived need, and indeed often where there was in fact none, as the old frontier was tamed and disappeared under the advancing rails. In the Rocky Mountains portion of Colorado, for example, the Denver & Rio Grande Railroad was just one, although the largest, of several railroads serving the region's mining towns. Much of the Denver & Rio Grande's track was originally built to the 36-in (0.914-m) gauge that became popular in the west after 1870, even though such narrow-gauge railroads possessed the inherent disadvantage of the impossibility of exchanging traffic with standard-gauge lines. The Denver & Rio Grande Railroad soon realized the error of its ways, however, and began the process of converting most of its track to standard gauge: the narrow-gauge branch between Durango and Silverton was preserved as a tourist attraction, however.

Yet there was still one more transcontinental line to be built. This fully characterized the waste typical of much railroad construction in the 19th century as it competed directly with two existing systems, yet became one of the most advanced American railroad operations. As noted above, Hill had been checked in his desire to secure control of the Chicago, Milwaukee & St. Paul Railroad as a complement to his transcontinental Great Northern and Northern Pacific routes, but had been able to gain control of the Chicago, Burlington & Quincy Railroad. The reaction of the board of the Chicago, Milwaukee & St. Paul Railroad to Hill's move was its 1905 decision to create the

OPPOSITE
Yuma, August 1877. The arrival of the first locomotive to Arizona.

LEFT
Boston & Maine's 4-4-0 locomotive (No. 525) hauls a passenger train, c. 1910.

BELOW LEFT
Manchester Locomotive Works 4-4-0 locomotive (No. 31) on the Fitchburg Railroad. The Fitchburg was leased by Boston & Maine from 1 July 1900, when this locomotive was given the Boston & Maine number 965. 1900.

July 4TH 1883

Road to its 1973 decision to abandon electric operations, which had proved a thoroughly economic exercise.

In the last quarter of the 19th century there were American railroads of every size, ranging from the upper limits of massive systems that measured their extent in thousands of miles to the lower limits of single-track lines only a few miles in length and operated by a single locomotive. Between these extremes there were specialized freight operators concentrating on the movement of just a single product such as coal, mineral ore, chemicals or lumber; and there were also suburban railroads providing short-distance transport into and out of cities for commuters.

What had become abundantly clear, over the same period, was that taken as a whole the railroad industry had become too important to the economic and social well-being of the U.S.A. to be left to the fluctuating desires of entrepreneurs and the ups and downs of the economy.

Analysis of the American railroad system in the last quarter of the 19th century reveals that the problems that had troubled many of the railroads were a direct result of the railroads' origins. Before the Civil War, the railroads were chartered by individual states, a fact that generally had a significant bearing on their routes. A typical example can be found in the Erie Railroad, which followed across the southern part of New York state – a route that was selected more for its relationship to the state border than for

OPPOSITE
The Atchison, Topeka & Santa Fe Railroad in the 1880s.

LEFT
Independence Day, 4 July 1883, saw this Chicago, Burlington & Quincy locomotive appropriately decorated for the occasion. The picture was taken at Aledo, Illinois. Behind the locomotive was a combination passenger, baggage, freight, and caboose car.

operator's own north-western route to the Pacific. Even though it had none of the land grants that had helped its predecessors complete their lines, the Chicago, Milwaukee & St. Paul Railroad managed to complete its line in only three years between Chicago and Seattle by a route shorter than those of either of its competitors. This success was achieved only at considerable cost and by following a route that included some very severe grades through several mountain ranges. As a result of the operational difficulties and challenges the railroad, which now added the word Pacific to its full title but which became known universally as the

Milwaukee Road, was persuaded to start an ambitious programme of electrification in the Rocky and Bitter Root Mountains. Two sections were equipped with an overhead supply of 3,000-volt DC current, that between Harlowtown and Avery being opened in 1917 and that between Othello and Seattle in 1920. Together they represented 656 miles (1056km) of electrified main line, the longest in the world at the time and using the most advanced system available. The eventual replacement of steam power by diesel locomotives, and the inconvenience of the 110-mile (177-km) interval between the two electrified sections, led the Milwaukee

Locomotive No. 999, a 4-4-0 of the New York Central Railroad's Empire State *express.*

By the end of the 19th century the American type of 4-4-0 locomotive, with its great funnel, was disappearing from service with the major railroads as more modern 4-4-0 units made their appearance to haul more advanced passenger and freight cars.

RIGHT
Randolph Street station, 1895.

BELOW RIGHT
Railroads played a key role in the industrial and agricultural development of the United States. This picture, from the late 19th century, shows freight cars loaded with cotton in St. Louis, Missouri railroad yards.

any practical consideration. Applied first to the transcontinental railroads and then to railroads in the territories that later became the western states, the land grant produced systems that were dependent on long-distance travel rather than local needs, and this produced the trend toward the merger of individual roads into interstate systems. This trend was initially left to the initiative of individual managements, resulting in operations that reflected the characters of their leaderships. Typical of this process was the Pennsylvania Railroad which, under the presidency of J. Edgar Thompson and then Thomas A. Scott, became probably the most efficient railroad system in the world: its track was the best, its locomotives were truly excellent, and its

The compartment-observation car of the Oriental Limited, *Chicago, Burlington & Quincy Railroad, in about 1910.*

CONSOLIDATION AND THE RAILROAD BARONS (1875–1917)

services superb. However, there were many operations that compared most unfavourably with the Pennsylvania Railroad, for the competition, or rather the nature of the competition, between the railroads, stemming from the emergence of interlocking systems, tended toward success as much through a great lack of scruples as through superb management capability.

Lack of scruples in management teams did at times have an adverse effect on investors, but often on the users of these railroads, who had to suffer the results of very poor safety standards, mainly in the continued use of unsafe track and thus frequent accidents.

The movement of freight was one of the operational aspects that had ramifications beyond mere freight transport. Competition in the rates charged for the movement of freight was derived from the two types of costs incurred by the railroads: the fixed costs of maintaining the system, and the running costs of moving a specific weight of load over a specific distance. On a route where there was a rival operator, it was tempting for a railroad to calculate its rates on the basis of running costs alone, leaving the fixed costs to be met from other sources, typically another route on which the same operator had a monopoly and could charge a higher rate. Another way in which the unscrupulous operator could seek to milk the market was in the charging of different rates for different commodities or for different journeys. This

meant that major customers, such as those moving large amounts of freight, could demand lower rates and, as long as they could cover their running costs, it was tempting for the railroads to satisfy these demands, even if it was merely to deprive a rival operator of the trade. In requiring the fixed costs to be met from other sources, however, the effect of this practice was the subsidization of the larger customer at the expense of the smaller. Where it faced no competition the railroad could charge whatever it thought it could get away with, and there were also the rate pools, in which rival railroads created a cartel that charged standard high rates to

avoid the costs of competition.

The type of customer which suffered most acutely from these and other abuses were farmers, who were wholly reliant on transport, and indeed on timely transport for their produce. In the circumstances, therefore, it is not surprising that it was the farmers who led the way in a resistance to these practices. In 1867, farmers had created an organization generally known as the National Grange, although it was more formally known as the Patrons of Husbandry. This was originally a social and educational body, but in the 1870s almost 1 million farmers, most of them in the Midwest, joined the

Interior of the old Santa Fe station at Lubbock, Texas, in 1911.

organization and the National Grange developed into a political force that coordinated the votes of its members to ensure the election of state legislators sympathetic to their cause, and thus the passing of laws to remove the most common abuses against farmers.

The railroads were another economic force well versed in the ways of controlling political and judicial processes for their own purposes. So the membership of the National Grange was most encouraged when railroad appeals against the new measures were dismissed by the Supreme Court. Then in 1886 the same court reversed its earlier decision,

issuing a judgement that states lacked the authority to regulate rates on traffic that passed beyond their own borders. This removed the primary legal plank on which the National Grange had developed its resistance to railroad pressure, and highlighted the steadily growing requirement for a federal solution to the problem.

The consolidation of individual routes into increasingly large systems, the process which had been the main cause of the competition leading to the rate wars, was speeded by the increasingly vociferous attacks heaped on the railroads. The process of consolidation in place of

confrontation between the railroads in the later part of the 19th century reached its decisive point in the person of J. Pierpont Morgan, the leading American banker of his day. Morgan had become involved in railroads during one of the skirmishes in the Erie wars, in the late 1860s. After reaching a compromise with Vanderbilt, Gould and Fisk had discovered the possibility of a new acquisition in the growing traffic from the coalfields of northern Pennsylvania. In 1869 a new link between Binghamton and Albany was about to be opened as the Albany & Susquehanna Railroad and, acting through the Delaware & Hudson Canal Company,

CONSOLIDATION AND THE RAILROAD BARONS (1875–1917)

An illustrative engraving of the Union Pacific Railroad. Sherman Summit, with an altitude of 8,013ft (2442m) is still one of the most famous railroad locations in the world.

Gould and Fisk tried to buy out the Albany & Susquehanna Railroad. However, there was sturdy opposition in the form of Morgan and the Lackawanna & Western Railroad. The inconclusive financial battle for control of the Albany & Susquehanna Railroad was finally ended in a trackside battle, in which the victory of Morgan's men persuaded Gould and Fisk to end their legal and political effort to seize control of the railroad.

The growth of his banking empire at the same time as the major development of the American railroad system inevitably drew Morgan toward railroad interests. By 1879 he was a director of the New York Central Railroad, and in 1880 was a leading figure in the raising of $40 million for the Northern Pacific Railroad in its time of dire need. With resources from private investors, or the local communities that were enabled by the 1869 General Bonding Law to raise money for the purchase of railroad securities, railroad construction in the 1870s had far outstripped demand: as noted elsewhere, many new lines were built without any realistic hope of immediate profitability, and by the end of the decade railroad bankruptcies were everyday events: 65 railroads, with a total capitalization of more than $200 million, went into liquidation in 1879 alone. Even those railroads that managed to avoid bankruptcy were faced with the situation in which they had to pay more than half of their income as interest on outstanding loans. No one seemed to learn from the implications of this fact, however, and every time the market had stabilized after a panic there developed another bout of uneconomic railroad construction.

One of the areas in which this tendency was most prevalent was New York, which by 1880 had more than 6,000

railroad's capabilities and so compel the existing operator to buy out the new railroad at an inflated price. In 1878, Vanderbilt had been forced to buy the new New York, Chicago & St. Louis Railroad as a means of protecting his Lake Shore route to Chicago, and in 1883 the West Shore Railroad began building up the Hudson in direct competition with the New York Central Railroad. Believing that the Pennsylvania Railroad was the force behind these moves onto what he believed to be his patch, Vanderbilt responded by buying the small but profitable coal-carrying Philadelphia & Reading Railroad as the basis for a new venture, the South Pennsylvania Railroad.

By 1885 Morgan's reputation as a railroad entrepreneur was suffering and it was decided that Vanderbilt and the Pennsylvania Railroad should buy each other's competing railroads, Vanderbilt taking over the West Shore and the Pennsylvania Railroad the South Pennsylvania Railroad. Morgan had the financial clout to impose this solution to the problem, and in the process took charge of reorganizing the South Pennsylvania, West Shore, and Philadelphia & Reading Railroads. In the process he became the owner of the South Pennsylvania Railroad to bypass the strictures of Pennsylvania state law prohibiting the Pennsylvania Railroad from buying competing railroads.

Like others, Morgan then found his railroad interest shifting to the west and, in common with earlier financiers with a

Cut-and-fill in the high sierras during the 1866 construction of the Central Pacific Railroad. This photograph shows the Chinese labourers with the one-horse carts they made famous.

miles (9655km) of track, with another 2,000 miles (3220km) added to this total by 1890. The level of competition was most strong between the major trunk routes. The New York Central and the Erie Railroads each included major networks of feeder lines, but faced competition from the Baltimore & Ohio and the

Pennsylvania Railroads for traffic to the Midwest. In the early 1880s the Pennsylvania Railroad was expanding very swiftly to the detriment of the other three operators.

There also emerged new railroads whose directors seemed to have no purpose but to duplicate an existing similar interest, found himself locked in conflict with other men of similar power and ambition. When trying to expand the Vanderbilt system from Chicago into Iowa, Morgan was checked by Edward Harriman, who had gained control of the Illinois Central Railroad in 1881 and had then shepherded it through prosperity in the direction of major expansion. The first clash between the two giants, over the obscure Dubuque & Sioux City Railroad in 1886, resulted in a victory for Harriman, but soon the two men were fighting over meatier bones.

In 1893 the Erie Railroad collapsed and, in restructuring the company, Morgan once again found himself in opposition to Harriman, who gained the upper hand and managed to impose some of his own conditions on the reorganization. Two years later, one of more than 150 railroads that failed was the Union Pacific Railroad; this operator's condition was by this time so poor that Morgan decided that it would not be sensible to attempt a resurrection, allowing Harriman, backed by Standard Oil, to take control. Within five years Harriman turned the Union Pacific Railroad into a highly successful operation, and on the 1900 death of Huntington paid $50 million to take control of the Southern Pacific Railroad.

In the interim, Morgan had forged an association with Hill to create a common ownership of the monopoly enjoyed by the Northern Pacific and Great Northern systems in the north-eastern part of the

U.S.A., and had also seen the Chicago, Burlington & Quincy Railroad added to this system. In New England, Morgan extended his control of the New York, New Haven & Hartford Railroad by taking over many of the smaller railroads in the area, and also used his influence to check the proposed expansion of the Philadelphia & Reading Railroad, which had now developed into a system with 5,000 miles (8045km) of track, until he himself had seized control of it. In the south-eastern part of the U.S.A., where the damage of the Civil War had been followed by constructors who took state funds but made little or no effort to build the railroads that these funds were to have funded, Morgan showed real flair in the creation of the 9,000-mile (14485-km) Southern Railways system.

Morgan was also able to maintain control over the complete network of New York trunk routes and their associated feeders, so that coal traffic was evenly distributed and uniform rates were charged.

Morgan had interests not only in the railroad arena, but also in a number of other major industrial areas, as typified by his part in the establishment of the huge U.S. Steel Trust. An industrial empire of this type can be maintained only on the basis of growth, and it was the search for growth in the railroad industry that bought Morgan to the final clash with that other giant, Harriman.

The area of conflict was the north-west part of the U.S.A., where the takeover of

the Chicago, Burlington & Quincy Railroad by James Hill, a supporter of Morgan, compelled Harriman into the implementation of an extraordinary plan in an effort to facilitate the entry to Chicago of his own Union Pacific-Southern Pacific system: when Hill refused to allow the sale to Harriman of part of the Chicago, Burlington & Quincy Railroad, Harriman decided to buy control of the Northern Pacific Railroad as a means of securing for himself its Chicago, Burlington & Quincy Railroad holdings.

There followed a huge financial battle between the money of Morgan and Hill on the one side, and that of Harriman, supported by Rockefeller, on the other: a battle of this type inevitably draws the attention of smaller interests who see the possibility of quick but nonetheless significant crumbs falling from the table of the giants. These smaller parties short-sold the rising stock of the Northern Pacific Railroad, but their plan had decidedly adverse effects as the price continued to rise and there was no stock available for purchase. This led to a financial panic requiring the two major parties to come to an agreement, and this led to establishment of a new holding company, in which both parties had an interest – the Northern Securities Corporation. This left the public out in the commercial cold, and pressure on the Congress led to the February 1888 passage of the Interstate Commerce Act through Congress. This act reversed the effect of the 1886 Supreme Court ruling in the matter of the National

Grange, and prohibited the establishment of pools; discriminatory rates; preferential treatment; and the full range of other common abuses; established that rates be just and reasonable; and created the Interstate Commerce Commission to supervise the full and equal implementation of the act's provisions. But the Interstate Commerce Commission lacked the teeth to enforce its decisions, and the public became completely disenchanted with the act after the decisions in 15 of the 16 rate cases brought to the Supreme Court between 1888 and 1905 went to the railroads.

The federal authorities had been slow to act in a number of other railroad-related matters: the standard gauge was not legally established until 1886; the Westinghouse air brake, which made possible huge improvements in operating efficiency as well as public safety, was adopted only hesitantly; and the universal coupling, another device which was eventually to save the lives of large numbers of railroad brakemen every year, was not made mandatory until 1893, the year in which air brakes were also required as a standard feature.

Finally, after the Northern Pacific Railroad affair of 1901, the federal authorities were finally forced into action. The railroads were themselves ready for legislation, for by this time in their histories, effects of the years of expansion and cut-throat competition were making themselves felt; the railroads were now suffering to an ever-increasing extent from

the type of abuse they had been all too willing to impose on their customers only a few years earlier: major customers, for example, could demand large and wholly secret reductions in the advertised freight rates.

The Elkins Act of 1903 strengthened the Interstate Commerce Act by making illegal any modification of the published rates without customers having to take court action to prove their case. The Hepburn Act of 1906 strengthened the Interstate Commerce Commission by extending the commission's powers to investigate and control all railroad activities, except those of a purely operational nature, enlarging it, giving it the power to fix maximum rates, and making its ruling binding.

In 1916 the eight-hour day was legally fixed as the standard, and in 1917 there was further intervention by the federal authorities. The eight-hour day increased the railroads' costs to an appreciable degree and this, combined with the Interstate Commerce Commission's refusal to allow any increase in freight rates, meant that the whole of the American railroad system was on the verge of commercial collapse in the period that followed the U.S.A.'s entry into World War I in April 1917. This period was marked by an enormous increase in the volume of railroad freight and men, equipment and a host of other supplies had to be moved to the ports of the American eastern seaboard for shipment to Europe. So parlous was the situation

that for a period of just over two years the federal authorities were forced to run the railroads.

The railroads passed back to their owners after this interval of government control, but now the conditions in which they had to operate were wholly different from those prevalent in the period before World War I. New forms of transport were on the verge of making major inroads into the market for mass transportation, and these inroads were reflected in the slow but steady diminution of the American railroad mileage from its peak of 250,000 miles (40232km) in 1916.

The construction of the track and a telegraph line through the Nevada desert in 1868. Central Pacific forces were building the western link of the first transcontinental railroad, now part of the Southern Pacific System. Rail-layers, shown in the foreground, were followed by gangs of Chinese labourers who spaced and spiked the rail to the ties.

CHAPTER FOUR

THE HEYDAY OF STEAM
(1917–1945)

By the time that the federal authorities took control of the railroads at the end of 1917, the beginning of the new era was evident in the fact that the giant figures of the previous era had disappeared or were leaving the scene: never again would the American railroad system see men of the vision and power, for good or bad, of Gould, Harriman, Hill, Morgan and Vanderbilt. Morgan had been the man who had made the greatest inroads into the problem of restructuring the American railroad system into a closer-linked and more effective whole, and it was on this concept that increasing federal legislation over the railroads began to build from the beginning of the 20th century. In part, this was the result of the Interstate Commerce Commission's work, and in part the belated recognition of the industry that it had to work on the basis of increasing cooperation, rather than steady antipathy within itself: as a result, the railroads had already begun to welcome the standardization of rates. The levels of

traffic, turnover and earnings more than doubled in the period between 1900 and 1913, but a depression in 1913–14 resulted in a modest lessening of traffic but a greater decrease in earnings. A large part of the problem was the excess of capacity over demand, and in 1914 and 1915 about 15,000 miles (24140km) of track were in receivership, and the fact that too much had been expended on the ownership revisions of the type in which the Pennsylvania Railroad had bought a large part of the Baltimore & Ohio Railroad and other north-eastern systems. The operator could then not afford to undertake the programme that was needed for the maintenance and replacement of its track and rolling stock, with the result that the traffic increase following the outbreak of World War I pushed the railroads to the limit and in some cases over it.

The main aspect of this failure was the breakdown of the logistical system that provided for freight cars hauled over other operators' tracks to be returned to their

owners. The massive increase in freight traffic to the north-eastern ports proved itself to be more than the railroads of this region could process and handle, resulting in a log jam of empty cars that severely hampered the unloading of newly arrived freight cars in New Jersey and New York, and also meant that freight operators in all other parts of the country began to run short of the freight cars they so desperately needed. The Railroad War Board was created in 1917 to solve this and other problems, but was so unsuccessful in its task that the federal authorities were forced to intervene and take over the task.

The operation of the railroads by the federal authorities became a matter of considerable controversy after the event, the adherents of private enterprise claiming that the efficiency of the railroad system had deteriorated under governmental control, that the concept of rerouting traffic from the Pennsylvania and the Baltimore & Ohio Railroads onto

Great Northern's L-class (2-6-6-2) locomotive, built by Baldwin in 1906–07, was an articulated Mallet.

the trunk routes in New York was fundamentally flawed, and that the property of the railroads had been wrongly neglected. The Director-General of Railroads contended, on the other hand, that overall efficiency had been enhanced by the standardization of operating procedures, and that the purchase of new equipment and compensation for the railroad operators was in fact a substantial federal subsidy.

It is impossible to establish which of these claims is the more accurate, but what cannot be denied is that price and wage inflation in the period up to 1920 had a very strong effect on the commercial viability of the American railroad network: this is indicated by the fact that in the period between 1914 and 1920, operating revenues doubled to $4 billion, while net income for the railroads dropped by a factor of 5 to $100 million. The new commercial realities of the period were reflected in the Transportation Act of 1920, which returned the railroads to their pre-war owners and also made provision for low-interest federal loans and grants to aid the reconstruction of the industry. The act also imposed on the Interstate Commerce Commission the obligation to create an overall plan for the consolidation of the American railroad network. The remit of the commission also included the obligation to allow the retention of existing routes, the preservation of competition, and the maintenance of uniform rates: denied the power to enforce mergers it thought necessary, the Interstate

Commerce Commission was in effect being instructed to plan a competitive system that had to come under monopoly conditions and then to bring this into existence with no powers but a right to veto mergers but not to force them. The overall effect, therefore, was to maintain the existing situation.

The Interstate Commerce Commission managed to develop such a plan, but successful opposition by the railroads scuppered any chances of it being activated. The railroads then began their own programme of consolidation, often employing arrangements that created mergers on a *de facto* rather than a *de iure* basis that gave the Interstate Commerce Commission no opportunity to use its veto power. In the north-eastern part of the U.S.A., for example, the Interstate Commerce Commission thought it desirable to create a fifth trunk route by rearrangements in the current Pennsylvania, New York Central, Baltimore & Ohio, and Erie Railroad systems with a consolidation of the Delaware, Lackawanna & Western and the Nickel Plate Railroads to balance the power of these five operators. The Pennsylvania and the New York Central Railroads, which would have been the major losers, successfully opposed the scheme but did not manage to come up with a viable alternative.

There were also changes in the ownership of several railroads. The Van Swerigen brothers bought a number of railroads, including the Nickel Plate in

OPPOSITE
Still redolent of an altogether different age is this 2-8-2 locomotive No. 487, built by Baldwin in 1925.

OPPOSITE
Construction of Pennsylvania station, New York. 1908.

LEFT
Horse-drawn taxis and 'tin lizzies' were familiar sights around Atlanta's Terminal station at the turn of the last century, and although they have been gone for years, Atlanta today, as then, is still served by the Southern Railway System.

THE HEYDAY OF STEAM (1917–1945)

In the U.S.A., as over much of Europe, there is still much private enthusiasm for the preservation and restoration of steam railroads for the edification of a public nostalgic for the sights, sounds and smells of an age that has otherwise passed into history. One such operation is the Tweetsie Railroad, one of whose locomotives is here caught by the camera.

1916 and the Erie in 1923. During 1924 the Pennsylvania Railroad secured a controlling interest in the Norfolk & Western Railroad, a major player in the coal transport business at Roanoke in Virginia. The Pennsylvania Railroad was doing well for itself, and also bought majority shareholdings in the Lehigh Valley, the Wabash and the Boston & Maine Railroads. The use of holding companies to bypass the regulations of the Interstate Commerce Commission was a practice also employed by the Van Swerigen brothers, who employed their Allegheny Corporation to develop a system of 30,000 miles (48280km); so useful was the ploy that holding companies created by the eastern trunk lines spent $300 million on purchases during 1928–29.

The situation was now beyond the control of the Interstate Commerce Commission, and the economic boom of the 1920s had proved so beneficial to their operations that the railroads forgot to plan against the contingencies that had so alarmed them in 1920. Route mileage dropped slightly from its maximum in 1916, but track mileage increased by some 100,000 miles (160930km) to 360,000 miles (579350km) in the course of 1928. Although they were now working in a corporate fashion rather than as the personal fiefs of private individuals, except in the case of the Van Swerigen bothers, the railroads now seemed to be on the verge of returning to the type of industry-shattering struggles that had caused so many problems in the past.

LEFT

Locomotive No. 3461, a 3460-class, Pacific-type 4-6-4, purchased from the Baldwin Locomotive Works in 1937. Boiler pressure was 300lb/sq in, there were 84-in drivers, and tender capacity was 20,000 gallons of water. Tractive effort was 43,000lb.

BELOW

Chicago, Burlington & Quincy steam locomotive No. 4960, a 2-8-2 Mikado (class O-1-A), built by the Baldwin Locomotive Works in 1923.

OPPOSITE
A Forney locomotive on the Manhattan Railroad's Third Avenue elevated in 1878.

LEFT
The Lake Street Elevated Railroad crossing over Oakley Boulevard , Chicago, in 1893.

Then came the great crash of 1929, and an early and badly hit part of the American economy was the railroad sector. Railroad revenues in 1930 were 15 per cent lower than in 1929, and by 1932 had declined to a mere 50 per cent of their 1929 level. By 1928 passenger miles had already dropped by 33 per cent from their 1920 level of 45 billion, largely as a result of the arrival on the transport scene of 15 million Ford Model T motor cars, and

further large falls were still to come.

The railroads reacted with the standard solutions of wage reductions, employee dismissals, and slashed dividends, while the federal authorities in 1932 created the National Transportation Committee that suggested cooperation to eliminate wasteful competition. In 1933, the new administration of President Franklin D. Roosevelt produced the Emergency Transportation Act, which

supported the recommendations of the National Transportation Committee and urged the creation of eastern, western and southern coordinating committees to help a Federal Transport Commissioner carry out the planned changes, though at the same time limited reductions in the labour force. In 1934 another important step was the establishment of the Association of American Railroads to act as a national policy-making body for the industry.

Valley-spanning bridges, such as that seen here on the operation of the Georgetown Loop Railroad, were among the greatest achievements of American civil engineering in the 19th century.

Wherever they still operate, trains hauled by steam locomotives are still an emotive draw for the American public. This is a sightseeing excursion in Hawaii by a train of the Lahaina, Kaanapali & Pacific Railroad.

RIGHT
A B-15-class Mogul at Hillsboro, New Hampshire on the Boston & Maine Railroad.

RIGHT
A B-15-class Mogul at Hillsboro, New Hampshire on the Boston & Maine Railroad.

BELOW RIGHT
A Denver & Rio Grande-class L-131-type 2-8-8-2 articulated locomotive, built by the Alco in 1927.

The Association of American Railroads and the Interstate Commerce Commission had soon reached agreement about several measures designed to improve the situation in what was now for many railroads a struggle for survival. Traffic levels were still falling, and by July 1938 no fewer than 39 major railroads (including the Van Swerigen holdings), with more than one-quarter of the U.S.A.'s total mileage between them, were in receivership.

On the recommendation of the Association of American Railroads, the Interstate Commerce Commission

suggested that interstate road traffic was brought under its control, although the further acceptance of rates parity was to prove something of a two-edged sword, having the effect, in many instances, of limiting the competitiveness of the railroads. The Interstate Commerce Commission also eased the railroads' debt obligations, the obtaining of federal loans, and the calls for public ownership.

As they emerged from the bleak years of the 1930s, the future of the railroads was eased by the 1940 Transportation Act, which went still further toward meeting their needs: the long-established requirement for the land-grant railroads to carry federal traffic at reduced rates was removed; water transport was added to the responsibilities of the Interstate Commerce Commission; it was announced that there was to be a non-competitive national transport policy, and there were fixed new rules for the Interstate Commerce Commission's system of approval for mergers. These last required the Interstate Commerce Commission to take into account both the interests of the public and the debt position of the railroads involved. The primary reason for the emollient treatment of the railroads during 1940 was federal concern about World War II, currently not involving the U.S.A. but spreading steadily and threatening ultimately to draw the U.S.A. into it. Should the U.S.A. become involved, the lessons of World War I demanded that the country possess a capable railroad network optimized for

LEFT
Boston & Maine's 0-6-0T switcher, Hampstead *(No. 240), was originally built for the Worcester, Nashua & Rochester Railroad before that line was leased to the Boston & Maine Railroad. 1890.*

OPPOSITE

American freight locomotives were seldom things of beauty, but they were very well engineered and constructed for a long life or effective service in one of the humdrum but profit-generating railroad roles.

LEFT

One of the primary reasons for the extension of the American railroad system into, rather than just through, the Great Plains was to service the meat industry. Cattle driven to the marshalling yards of cities such as Abilene, Kansas, were fattened locally and then shipped to the great meat-packing centres of cities such as Chicago, Illinois.

A 3800-class Santa Fe-type 2-10-2 locomotive, built by the Baldwin Locomotive Works, hauling a freight train through Cajon Pass, California.

LEFT

A Union Pacific 4-8-4 FEF. 2 800-class passenger & freight locomotive, introduced into service in 1939.

BELOW LEFT

Norfolk & Western Class A articulated engine 1201, built at Roanoke, Virginia in 1936.

One of the truly great names and institutions of the American railroad system is the Union Pacific Railroad. This was partially responsible for the creation of the first transcontinental railroad, building its line and service eastward from the U.S.A.'s Pacific seaboard.

Though it could hardly be described as environmentally friendly by the standard prevailing in the early part of the 21st century, trains hauled by powerful steam locomotives were nonetheless highly impressive entities as a result of their sheer presence.

RIGHT

*Santa Fe's Class 2900 4-8-4
locomotive. One of 30 oil-
burners, with driving wheels
80-in (0.68-m) in diameter,
the tender had a capacity of
25,000 gallons of water and
7,000 gallons of oil.*

BELOW RIGHT

*A Union Pacific 4-6-6-4
Challenger-class (CSA-class
designation) locomotive, the
first of a type built in 1942
for freight and passenger
services.*

OPPOSITE

*Locomotive 5000, a 5000-
class Santa Fe-type 2-10-4,
purchased from Baldwin in
1930.*

OPPOSITE
Union Pacific No. 4002, a 4-8-8-4 Big Boy-class articulated steam locomotive built in 1941.

LEFT
Santa Fe's Class 3460 Pacific-type 4-6-4. Built by the Baldwin Locomotive Works in 1937, it had 84-in diameter driving wheels and a tender capacity of 20,000 gallons of water.

personnel and freight movements over long distances at high speeds.

The U.S.A. was indeed drawn into World War II, in this instance in December 1941 as a result of the Japanese attack on Pearl Harbor and other American interests in and around the Pacific Ocean, and the railroads once again became a key element of the rapidly expanded U.S. war effort. Apart from a token three-week nationalization of the railroads at the end of 1944 to head off the possibility of labour problems, the railroads worked extremely capably throughout the U.S.A.'s involvement in the war, and cooperated excellently with the Office of Defense Transportation. This rendered superfluous any possible repetition of the type of drastic action that had been required in 1917, and as a consequence the movement of war materiel and personnel to port

areas followed by the extraction of the empty cars worked well, avoiding the wholesale levels of congestion that had partially crippled the movement of men and equipment to France in World War I.

The railroads themselves used the situation to reveal the growing level of financial maturity that they had attained, for instead of disbursing the greater profits generated by the movement of war traffic on large dividends, they used the money to trim the fixed charges for interest on debts. This marked a radical departure for the railroad operators, for debt had been a millstone round the neck of the railroads' financial flexibility almost since their beginnings. Up to this time, debts had been seen as permanent fixtures, but now a major effort was being made toward the reduction of the debt burden, whose annual charges were

reduced by about $80 million between 1940 and 1945. This effort was to yield useful results in the post-war years, when the railroads' newly created financial 'credibility' made it simpler for them to raise the $2 billion they then needed for the large-scale dieselization that was emerging as the railroads' preferred option to replace coal-fired locomotion.

Other factors in the post-war years were less favourable for the railroads. By 1946 their income had already fallen by 10 per cent compared with that of 1944, and passenger traffic was declining dramatically. By 1950 the railroads' share of passenger mileage for journeys between cities rather than in and around them was under 50 per cent of the national total, with buses taking nearly 40 per cent; but the buses' share also declined from that point as the importance of air travel

Black Diamond, *the Lehigh Valley Railroad streamliner, operating between Norfolk and Buffalo.*

New York Central's 4-6-4 Hudson *streamlined locomotive, used to haul the* Empire State *express. 1930s.*

increased. By 1960 buses and trains were each carrying about 25 per cent of the total, while the airlines were carrying 40 per cent; by 1970 the airlines accounted for more than 75 per cent of the total. After the railroads' drastic reduction of passenger services in the early 1970s, even private aircraft logged a greater number of passenger miles than the railroads. It is worth remembering, though, that all other

forms of public intercity transport had been overtaken by the private motor car as early as the 1920s, but nonetheless it was gloomy news for the railroads that by the mid-1970s all forms of public transport combined (and in this the railroads accounted for only a very small proportion) and were transporting just a miserable 13 per cent.

Over the same period, the analysis of

freight traffic also reveals that there was a steady decline in railroad freight within the context of the total freight business in the U.S.A. From a figure of almost 70 per cent in 1944, the railroads of the freight market declined to 56 per cent by 1950, 44 per cent by 1960, and less than 40 per cent during the 1970s: over the same period, trucks carried more than 20 per cent from 1960, canals and rivers more than 10 per

OPPOSITE
*A-class 4-4-2 steam
locomotives.*

LEFT
*A Norfolk & Western
Railroad 4-8-4 J-class
locomotive, heading an
express passenger train. Late
1940s.*

cent by 1970, and oil pipelines almost 25 per cent. Actual freight tonnages moved by the railroads were slightly greater in the mid-1970s than they had been in 1944, but during the period the overall freight tonnage had doubled.

There was only a little that the railroads could do in their efforts to halt this tendency. The introduction of diesel power had the advantage of boosting

efficiency but also required a huge investment of scarce capital. Higher levels of mechanization and automation also offered the probability of enhanced operational efficiency, but once more the required capital outlay was too much for virtually every railroad to contemplate. Diversification into other areas of activity also provided an alternative source of revenue, but of course lack of success in

any new area could not only add to but in fact also exacerbate current difficulties. One solution tried by a number of the railroads experiencing difficulties in the period after World War II was a reversion to the 'old way', namely merger and/or consolidation. The approval of the Interstate Commerce Commission was still required for any such move, and the improvement in a railroad's chances of

OPPOSITE and LEFT
The 1920s and 1930s saw the widespread development and use of 'streamliners', as these carefully shaped steam locomotives were called, in an effort to boost speed while reducing cost through the reduction in drag. The effort also produced visually impressive and therefore popular locomotives such as the Chicago & North Western Railroad's E4-class (left) and F7-class (opposite) 4-6-4 locomotives, the former caught by the camera near Milwaukee, Wisconsin, in 1938.

survival was not one of the primary criteria that the Interstate Commerce Commission took into account in its reckonings. Nevertheless, a number of mergers were and have been accomplished with some success for the parties involved.

In 1959, for example, the Norfolk & Western Railroad merged with the Virginian Railroad in a combination of two operators whose primary interests lay in the movement of coal and which brought complementary track layouts into the merger. The 1960 amalgamation of the Erie

& Delaware Railroad with the Lackawanna & Western Railroad opened the way for the duplication of track to be eliminated, offering the possibility of considerable savings in maintenance and operating costs; but the early financial results of the new Erie-Lackawanna Railroad were worse than the two companies' losses before their merger. On a larger scale, the Chesapeake & Ohio Railroad's takeover of the Baltimore & Ohio Railroad created another major coal-carrying system extending from Chesapeake Bay to the Great Lakes and,

by means of the Chesapeake & Ohio Railroad's earlier purchase of the Père Marquette Railroad, into Canada proper. The Seaboard Air Line and Atlantic Coast Line merged their east coast systems in 1967 to produce the Seaboard Coast Line, while the later purchase of the Louisville & Nashville Railroad and the leasing of other southern railroads served to extend the network of the new Family Lines System from Miami and Washington, D.C., in the east to New Orleans, Memphis, St. Louis and Chicago in the west. The merger that came as the greatest surprise

New York Central Railroad 4-6-4 Hudson-class locomotive, streamlined to head the Twentieth Century Limited. *Photographed in March 1938 at the Alco plant.*

to all those interested in American railroad affairs was that of the old rivals, the Pennsylvania and the New York Central Railroads in the course of 1968. For a variety of reasons, including the residues of long-standing antipathies between the two well established corporate regimes and an inability to make full use of the possibilities for consolidation and elimination of duplication, the new Penn-Central Railroad went into bankruptcy in 1970. Other railroads that failed in the same dire period for the American railroad system included the Ann Arbor, Boston & Maine, Erie-Lackawanna, Lehigh Valley, Central of New Jersey, and Reading Railroads, all of which could blame their demise on the drastic lessening of the coal traffic required in the New York area.

The failures of nearly all the railroads of the north-eastern region of the U.S.A. was an event that needed swift and strong action on the part of the federal authorities if the malaise was not to spread from the railroads to the industries and communities these railroads served, and this prompted the 1973 Rail Reorganization Act. This created the U.S. Railroad Association as a wholly representative organization whose task it was to plan the creation of a rationalized network of the type that the Interstate Commerce Commission had not been permitted to establish some half a century earlier, and also created Conrail (the Consolidated Rail Corporation) to run the system that emerged from the U.S. Railroad Association's deliberations. When

Conrail began operations in the course of 1976 with a subsidy of $6 billion, it was the second biggest operator of its type in the U.S.A., but the financial haemorrhaging typical of the railroad industry during this period meant that before 1980 it had returned to the federal authorities with a request for additional subsidies: only with these, Conrail informed the federal authorities, could it hope to overcome the railroad industry's core problems of out-dated and worn-out equipment as well as very high operating costs.

Despite the size and potential cost it represented, Conrail was not the only, or indeed the first, part of the railroad industry to demand and receive support from the federal authorities. The first of these parts to fail, in the later part of the 1960s, had been the intercity passenger services, and their collapse necessitated a major undertaking by the federal authorities: the operators of the surviving intercity services had to decide between handing over their passenger rolling stock and locomotives, as well as a cash sum based on their anticipated losses, to a new National Railroad Passenger Corporation operating under the name Amtrak, and continuing their passenger services under their own names for a period of at least two years. So difficult was the situation of the intercity passenger services that the vast majority of them opted from the Amtrak solution, the only major stand-outs being the Southern Railroad's *Southern Crescent* service linking

LEFT

Beaver Tail car on the Chicago, Milwaukee, St. Paul & Pacific Railroad Company's Hiawatha *express in 1935.*

Southern Pacific's 4-8-4 Daylight-class locomotive, heading a streamliner between San Francisco and Los Angeles in 1936.

Washington, Atlanta and New Orleans, and the Denver & Rio Grande Western Railroad's *Zephyr* service. Even then, during 1979, the Southern Railroad's outlook was so bad, with annual losses of $7 million or thereabouts, that it yielded and joined the Amtrak system.

The new operator of intercity passenger operations, Amtrak could not start afresh, but inherited a mass of difficulties including antiquated rolling stock that had to be operated over track it did not control. With mounting losses, its future looked bleak until the fuel crisis of

1979 persuaded the Congress not to vote for President Jimmy Carter's planned reductions in services and funding but rather to boost Amtrak's subsidy by 50 per cent; then progress was made in the process of updating the North-East 'corridor' link between Boston and Washington, which Conrail was forced to hand over, with new rolling stock.

Throughout the 1970s conventional mergers also continued. The decade's first year witnessed the ultimately inevitable consolidation of the old Hill railroad holdings in the north-west of the

country as the Chicago, Burlington & Quincy, the Great Northern, the Northern Pacific, and the Spokane, Portland & Seattle Railroads were brought together as the Burlington Northern Railroad, the most substantial network of railroads in the USA. The Interstate Commerce Commission denied the plans of the Milwaukee Road and Rock Island Line to merge with the Union Pacific Railroad and Chicago & North Western Railroads respectively, and the first two operators went out of business. There were proposals at various levels for the establishment of a western equivalent of Conrail, but the probable cost to the nation persuaded the federal authorities against any such undertaking. This left the Interstate Commerce Commission to rule on the attempts of the Southern Pacific Railroad's bid to buy the section of the Rock Island Line's network between New Mexico and St. Louis, in the face of objections from the Santa Fe.

The problem faced by the Interstate Commerce Commission in looking at these and other mergers planned for the 1980s (such as the planned merger of the 'Chessie System', as the Chesapeake & Ohio Railroad was generally known, and the Family Lines, and the possible unions involving the Union Pacific, Missouri Pacific and Western Pacific Railroads)

were the difficult if not impossible tasks of securing balance. On the one side there were the legitimate expectations of private enterprise, and on the other the needs of the nation, in social and economic terms, from a huge industry that had developed in a piecemeal and sporadic way under the guiding hand of no one authority.

The best example available to American railroad operators is perhaps Union Pacific Railroad, although this exists and operates in a somewhat atypical way that perhaps or even probably makes emulation of its capabilities difficult for others. The Union Pacific Railroad was at one time believed to be past the point of no return as its fortunes waned, but it has been turned round to re-emerge from the financial and operational doldrums as a

fine example of operational efficiency and financial success. The Union Pacific Railroad is fortunate in possessing interests outside its railroad operations, in fields such as coal and oil that are money-making in themselves and also provide revenue-generating traffic for the Union Pacific Railroad's modern railroad. Moreover, the level of investment necessary to bring any less prosperous railroad up to the same technical level of excellence as the Union Pacific Railroad is probably beyond even the dreams of anything but a national organization, private or public. The Union Pacific Railroad's operation is characterized by a very high qualitative level of track, rolling stock, motive power and computerized control.

A Union Pacific 4-6-6-4 Challenger-class 'C5A' locomotive, first of the type built in 1936 for freight and passenger operations.

CHAPTER FIVE
BUILDING THE ROADS

The early American railroads were among the first in the world, and from their beginnings were the longest that had yet been planned. The pioneering American railroad engineers had to evolve the appropriate basic construction techniques virtually by trial and error, and had also to face particular problems of their own. For example, in the absence of any indigenous capability for the manufacture and working of iron in industrially-large quantities, the American railroad companies had to import the rail they required, usually from the U.K. Heavy engineering was also an infant in the U.S.A., though inventive individuals quickly created the designs for locomotives and other equipment which rapidly came to possess a distinctively American nature. The most immediate problem, however, was the fact that as soon as they had headed away from the settled coastal regions of the U.S.A., the builders had to create the railroads in largely unknown territory that had, as a

wholly essential first stage, to be surveyed as a means of finding the right route.

Surveying was completed in stages. The essential first stage was a visual reconnaissance by the engineer-in-chief to establish the general direction that the railroad would take. Then came the process of instrument surveying, with a lead flagman to mark out the approximate route being followed by the transitman, a team to record the distances and angles that were involved, and the leveller, who measured the elevations and inclines of the selected routes. At the same time,

OPPOSITE
Freight operations, now of an advanced nature, including flatcars optimized for the single- or double-deck movement of preloaded containers, are a key element in the continued viability of railroad operators in Canada as well as the U.S.A. These are Canadian National Railway Company operators at the important port of Halifax, Nova Scotia.

LEFT
After a major slump in its fortunes, especially during the third quarter of the 20th century, the American railroad industry has been undergoing a considerable rebirth in terms of its technical and commercial success. The continued importance of freight operations underpins much of this renaissance, but passenger traffic is also improving and these two factors have made it possible for operators such as Conrail to introduce revised equipment.

RIGHT

Section gangs, like this Chicago, Burlington & Quincy crew, rode the rails on handcars to replace rotted ties, tamp loose spikes and tighten bolts. As a memento of their shared sense of responsibility, they struck this pose in the 1870s. Their foreman's solemn little daughter is in a place of honour.

OPPOSITE,
ABOVE LEFT

Construction work on Cut No. 1 west of the Narrows, Weber Canyon. The Narrows are situated 4 miles (6.5km) west of Echo and 995 miles (1600km) west of Omaha and presented some of the most difficult grading in the building of the Union Pacific Railroad. Successive shelves were hacked into rock, then pickaxed and blasted down to grade. Rough, temporary tracks were laid to take the rubble away, while mules and carts did the job on higher levels.

BELOW LEFT

Bunkie, Lousiana, a station of the Southern Railroad.

other teams were clearing trees and undergrowth, and a topographer would also be employed to make a visual record of the landscape, including hills and rivers that could have a bearing on the ultimate choice.

This orderly process had to be adapted to the circumstances of the particular project in question, of course, and when the Americans started seriously to consider the question of transcontinental railroads, the process became altogether larger and considerably more complex. When the realization of the idea of creating a transcontinental railroad was emerging from a theoretical concept toward a practical possibility in the course of the 1850s, the U.S. Army's Corps of Engineers undertook a series of surveys.

ABOVE

This passenger station was the first in Minneapolis. The railroad was the St. Paul & Pacific and was also the first in the North-West. It ran from St. Paul to Minneapolis (then known as St. Anthony).

RIGHT

Bulk operations often demand the creation of special facilities. This is part of the ore-loading operation facility at the single-purpose dock near Duluth.

OPPOSITE

A Northern Pacific construction crew.

The Pioneer *was the first locomotive in Chicago. Used by the Galena & Chicago Union, she had to be carried to the city by sailing vessel on the Great Lakes because there were no tracks to the east at that time. A light engine, she was soon relegated to construction train work, as shown here on the bridge over the Rock river at Rockford, Illinois, in 1869. The engine still survives as one of the oldest remaining in the U.S.A.*

After nearly a year, the corps produced 13 illustrated volumes of reports on the country they had examined, though it has to be admitted that the details of the information presented in these volumes was more concerned with the geography of the Far West than the establishment of a practical railroad route.

The route that was finally adopted was that surveyed by Theodore Judah and his employers of the Southern Pacific Railroad. Yet even this initially planned route was varied in accordance with the willingness or otherwise of the communities along the way to contribute to the cost of the railroad's construction. And while the route of the Union Pacific Railroad from the east was generally that

of the old Mormon Trail to Utah, the surveyors and construction teams had to bear in mind throughout that trails passable with ox-teams and horse-drawn wagons were very often unsuitable for the purposes of railroad operations.

One of the primary obstacles to the westward advance of the Union Pacific Railroad was the Black Hills spur of the Rocky Mountains between Cheyenne and Laramie in the southern part of Wyoming. Grenville Dodge, who had commanded in the U.S. Army's campaigns against the Native Americans in 1865–66 in this area, before being appointed chief engineer of the Union Pacific Railroad, gathered detailed reports on the region and also explored it himself during this time, but

Trestle bridges are still very much part of the American railroad scene, and while many of these are tall structures spanning high but comparatively narrow valleys, a not inconsiderable number are low structures of considerable length. Typical of this latter type is the bridge at Modesto, California, seen here with a freight train of the Southern Pacific Railroad crossing over it.

had little success in finding the right type of gap accessible from the east until a chance encounter with some Native Americans proved to be the breakthrough he was seeking. During one journey, Dodge and a small party of men were passing south along the crest of the range from the Cheyenne Pass while the main body of his command, returning from the Powder river expedition, continued along the trail at the foot of the mountains. Then cut off from the main body by a Native American band, Dodge and his small party managed to fight their way down from the crest and chanced on a ridge which formed an unbroken line down to the plains below. It was the perfect route over the mountains and the Union Pacific Railroad then crossed over the Black Hills by this pass, which Dodge named after his old commander, General Sherman. The summit of the pass, lying at an altitude of more than 8,000ft (2440m), was the highest altitude reached by an American railroad up to that time.

About 20 years later, the builders of the Canadian transcontinental railway faced severe natural barriers, and the country through which the railway had to pass was even less known than that faced by the American railroad pioneers in their efforts to drive the lines through the Great Plains and Rocky Mountains. British Columbia offered the possibility of two ends for the new railway, on the Burrard and the Bute inlets from the Georgian Sea: the former lies at the mouth of the Fraser river, which forms a natural entry to the

*The physical nature of the
U.S.A., with major
mountain ranges in the east
and most particularly in the
west, in the Rocky
Mountains and associated
chains, required major
engineering efforts to create
switchbacks, bridges and
tunnels. The last is here
exemplified by the Moffat
Tunnel on the network of the
Southern Pacific Railroad.*

Baltimore & Ohio Railroad employees from the locomotive and freight car repair shops at Grafton, West Virginia.

Coastal mountain range and had been used for this purpose during the gold rush of 1858, while the latter was less well known but was a potential site for a bridge to Vancouver Island and the provincial capital of Victoria. Farther inland, the course of the Fraser turns north, with the Thompson river flowing into it from the east at Lytton. Up the Thompson river lies Kamloops Lake, and beyond this is Eagle Pass, but there remained the Selkirk and Rocky ranges still to be crossed before the projected railway line could be built to the east. Yellowhead Pass had been used by gold prospectors from the east in 1858, and was the course preferred by Sandford Fleming,

the engineer-in-chief, while the discoverer of Eagle Pass had recommended Howse Pass, reached from Eagle Pass by a northward sweep of the Columbia river. Far to the north, other surveys had located Pine River Pass that could be reached by means of the valley of the Fraser river.

The first contracts issued by the government of Canada for railway construction in British Columbia, signed in 1880, demanded a course running from Burrard Inlet up the old gold route to Kamloops, and in the following year the Canadian Pacific Railway Company was established for the construction of the main transcontinental railway. All the routes previously considered had involved

long detours to the north, with the Yellowhead Pass route offering the easiest grades, but James Hill, one of the original directors of the Canadian Pacific Railway Company, was unhappy with this and demanded further surveys in the region south of Howse Pass.

Of two other likely routes, the more southerly Kootenay Pass was uncomfortably close to the border between Canada and the U.S.A., especially at a time when war between the two was a possibility if not a probability. The route north of Howse Pass was longer, and would also expose Canada's southern prairie region, both open to 'infiltration' by the railroads being built in the north-western part of the U.S.A., and to the

annexation demanded by many American politicians at the time. Hill decided, probably in advance, that the Bow river route through Kicking Horse Pass would be adopted, and Hill offered Major A.B. Rogers, the company's new surveyor, a bonus if he could find a usable Kicking Horse Pass route. Rogers found the way, through the pass named for him, but he exacerbated the construction programme by underestimating the grades of this route.

Even after fortune, politics and financial considerations had combined to fix the general course of the new railway, the planners still had to undertake the labour of precise measurement. Fleming's first surveys for the Canadian

RIGHT

The Techahapi/Walong Loop reveals one of the expedients to which railroad engineers have recourse in their efforts to create a means of reducing gradients to an acceptable figure. Here the looping of the track with one leg passing under the other allows a manageable gradient.

BELOW

One type of severe weather condition which railroad engineers have to cope with in their planning, is neatly encapsulated in this photograph of a tunnel entrance.

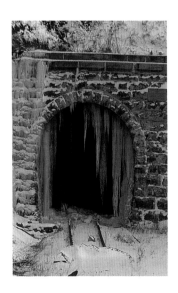

The boring of Northern Pacific Railroad's 9,850-ft (3000-m) Stampede Tunnel in the Cascade range of Washington Territory was conducted on two levels and from the eastern and western slopes of the mountain from February 1886 to May 1888. The West's first electric power plant was built expressly to lighten the work of construction. This also marked the introduction of Ingersoll air-operated drilling equipment to that part of the country. The tunnel was completed several days ahead of schedule and the first train rolled through it on 12 May 1888, permanently linking the Great Lakes with Puget Sound. Stampede Tunnel is in regular use today, more than 100 years later.

OPPOSITE

Construction forces of the St. Paul, Minneapolis & Manitoba Railroad, accompanied by soldiers for protection from hostile Native Americans. This 1887 photograph was taken in what today is western North Dakota but which was then Dakota Territory. The railroad was being extended that year from Minot to Great Falls and Helena, in Montana Territory, and four world records were established in the process. Construction began just west of Minot on 2 April and reached Helena 642-miles (1030-km) distant on 19 November. The 'Skyscraper' dormitory cars shown here had to be sawn down to tunnel size when the rails reached the mountains.

ABOVE

A Northern Pacific Railroad gang laying track in western Dakota, 1880.

transcontinental route had involved 2,000 men or more, and of the 46,000 miles (74025km) of possible route reconnoitred on foot, some 11,500 miles (18505km) had to be covered by detail surveying teams.

In the standard system for laying out the route for a new railroad or railway, assuming there could ever have been such a system, the chief engineer would use the information gathered by the instrument surveying party for the final

determination of the route to be built. This decision might be based on the chief engineer's opinion as the option most likely to provide the easiest course, or on his belief that established towns or the location of physical features, such as mountain passes or bridging points on rivers, offered the best possibilities. Often, though, the chief engineer's decision might be made for him by the nature of the region, such as a mine in a

mountainous area to be reached, which often meant the adoption of the only possible course regardless of adverse factors.

The selection of the new railroad's line was, of course, of critical importance: while it was possible for poor construction work to be remedied at a later and less pressured time, the initial adoption of the wrong decision could mean that an already constructed line had to be

abandoned and the section of line in question be created from scratch once more. The two most decisive elements in the chief engineer's selection of the route were the steepness of the grades and the sharpness of the curves.

The severity of grades gave the chief engineer little scope for trade-offs. The fact that there is a low coefficient of friction between a smooth metal wheel and a smooth metal rail makes for efficiency of operation on the level, where a typical 40-ton car moving at a steady 60mph (97km/h) rolls to a halt only after about 5 miles (8km), but also reduces the locomotive's tractive effort and imposes a severe limit on the gradient the locomotive can climb before its driving wheels start to slip; even where a locomotive can climb a

A major key to the effective, and therefore profitable, operation of any railroad is the creation of a system and its associated facilities for the location of the right train in the right place at the right time. This is the task carried out in marshalling yards of the type seen here, the Colton Yard of the Southern Pacific Railroad.

RIGHT
Construction of the Northern Pacific Railroad at Big Rock Cut, one mile above Cabinet.

OPPOSITE
Snow was piled high at trackside in the Cascade Mountains on 6 January 1893, when two Great Northern Railway officials drove the final spike into a roughly-hewn cross tie to complete a continuous track from the Twin Cities of Minnesota to Puget Sound. Pomp and ceremony were ignored as workmen on the track-laying rig lowered the last rails onto ties. James. J. Hill, Great Northern's founder, who pushed the lines across prairies, along river valleys and over the Rockies, was not there for the historic event. As the heavy hammer pounded the last spike, cheers rose from the workmen. They were drowned out by the sharp cracks from a six-shooter and the shrill whistles of work train locomotives that reverberated throughout the Skykomish Valley.

RIGHT

The large tug 'Sally J' passes under the open Burlington Northern Railroad bridge across Salmon Bay, Seattle, Washington.

OPPOSITE

The North American continent is criss-crossed by myriad rivers and other watercourses, vast numbers of which have had to be bridged in one way or another to allow the creation of a comprehensive continental railroad network. This is the Revelstoke crossing of the Columbia river on the network of the Canadian Pacific Railway Company, whose operations demanded the creation of bridges over tidal waters and river courses that were sometimes wide and shallow and in other places narrow and deep, often subject to widely differing water quantities and speeds at different times of the year.

gradient, its ability to haul a significant weight is severely limited.

In overall terms, the American railroads approved sharper curves than their equivalents in Europe: in the U.S.A. a curve with a radius of 300ft (91.5m) was relatively common, while in Europe a main-line curve with a radius of less than 1,000ft (305m) was generally not allowable. The tightness of the curves on American railroads was one of the primary reasons for the development and adoption of the pivoted pilot truck and equalized driving wheel suspension of the American standard locomotive that was adopted universally in the early years of

the railroads. It should be noted, however, that a major speed penalty was dictated by the permissibility of tight curves.

Yet the chief engineer has to take into account the fact that the construction of track that is optimized for haulage by being straight and level almost certainly demands far greater constructive effort in driving cuttings through hills and filling hollows with embankments or viaducts. The labour of these tasks was reduced by the introduction of the first powered construction equipment, in the form of the steam shovel, and was then simplified further by the development of more modern mechanized earth-moving

ABOVE
The wooden trestle bridges typical of the first American railroad operations were later replaced by more durable structures of iron and then steel. This is a metal bridge on one of the Burlington Northern Railroad's lines.

OPPOSITE
A freight train passes along the track laid on an embanked causeway, constructed over a stretch of slow-moving water.

171

The Baltimore & Ohio rail bridge at the junction of the Potomac and Shenandoah rivers at Harper's Ferry, West Virginia in the 1920s.

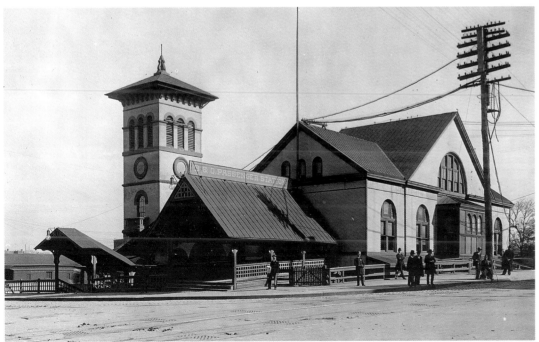

equipment; but this could not alter the inevitable fact that cutting and filling added to construction cost. In overall terms, therefore, the art that characterized the great railroad engineers was their ability to balance the conflicting factors of construction cost and operational efficiency. Compromises of this type were very typical of American railroad construction in the 19th century, when the standard principle became the selection of the correct route and the construction of the track as quickly and cheaply as possible, with detours round obstacles readily accepted even if this made the line longer or less amenable to higher operating speeds. Only then, once trains were operating and revenue was being generated, was it the time to improve the track and enhance the route.

The classic example of this latter concept was the elimination of the original meeting point of the Union Pacific and Central Pacific Railroads at Promontory in Utah: during 1904 the Southern Pacific Railroad, as successor to the Central Pacific Railroad, constructed a new 132-mile (212-km) line across the Great Salt Lake, in the process trimming 44 miles (71km) off the original route and missing Promontory, and at the same time avoiding a number of severe grades and sharp curves. In 1967 the Southern Pacific Railroad took another chokepoint out of its system by constructing a new line between Palmdale in California and the classification yard at Colton. Freight from the north-western part of the U.S.A.

LEFT
Graceful curves and fancy trimming predominated in the architectural design of passenger stations by the predecessor of the Southern, the South Carolina Railroad. A typical example is this station and freight shed built by South Carolina Railroad at Summerville, South Carolina, sometime in the 1880s, but dismantled in 1935.

BELOW LEFT
Baltimore & Ohio Railroad's passenger station at New Jersey Avenue, Washington, D.C. in the late 1800s.

RIGHT

Three switch engines and their crew pose in front of the former station at Pacific Junction, Iowa in 1905. This is where the Kansas City-Council Bluffs line crosses the main line to Lincoln, and where trains for Council Bluffs and Omaha can turn north and follow the Missouri.

BELOW

A one-car Northern Pacific train, with wood-burning balloon stack locomotive, is shown here at the end of the bridge over the Missouri river between Bismarck and Mandan, Dakota Territory.

travelling toward the southern portions of the railroad had previously been compelled to pass right through Los Angeles on the original line through the San Joaquin valley: to reduce delay, therefore, the new line from Palmdale through the Cajon Pass to Colton, comprising 78 miles (126km) of new main line and 12 miles (19.3km) of associated sidings, was built in a mere 15 months with the aid of the most modern construction equipment.

Another notable but earlier improvement of this nature, known as a cut-off, was effected by the Denver & Rio Grande Western Railroad to trim the distance between Denver and the west via

Salt Lake City. The original route involved a lengthy swing to the south via Pueblo, but the 1928 completion of the 6.2-mile (10-km) Moffat Tunnel between Bond and Dotsero allowed the activation of the Dotsero cut-off, cutting 65 miles (105km) from the journey.

In 1929 the Cascade Tunnel, on the Great Northern Railway's line through the Cascade mountain range in Washington state, was completed as the longest tunnel in the U.S.A. This was the second major improvement on this section of the Great Northern Railway's line after a 2.6-mile (4.2-km) tunnel was completed in 1900 to avoid the original switchbacks through the mountains. The line still had severe

In its eagerness to push toward Utah in its race with the westward building of the Union Pacific, Central Pacific bridged many of the High Sierra chasms with timber trestles. When the railroad was completed, they came back and the Chinese labourers who had built the railroad filled them in with solid earth and embankments. This remarkable photograph was taken at Secrettown Trestle, 62 miles (100km) from Sacramento on the western slope of the Sierra in 1877. Scrapers were not in use as yet for grading. Dynamite had been invented but was not in general use. The Chinese used picks and shovels, chisels and hammers, black powder, wheelbarrows and one-horse dump carts.

approach grades, however, and with the
competition of the Milwaukee Road on the
line to Seattle, the Great Northern Railway
began another step in its programme of
improvement: this resulted in the 7.8-mile
(12.6-km) Cascade Tunnel, the
electrification of some 71 miles (114km) of
track, and a 10-mile (16-km) reduction in
the overall distance through elimination of
several miles of snowsheds, older tunnels
and grades of more than 2 per cent.

The most radical of improvements of
this type is probably to be found on the
Canadian Pacific Railway Company's main
line over Kicking Horse Pass. From the
east, 7 miles (11.25km) of grades more
acute than 4 per cent down into the
Columbia river valley led to a
comparatively level extent and then
another length of 2.2 per cent grades up to
Rogers Pass. In the period of steam
locomotion this meant that as many as
three locomotives were necessary to move
only eight cars. Avalanches were a danger
in winter, and both time and money were
lost in the negotiation of the miles of loops
leading up to and down from the summit.
The first step in the improvement
programme was the driving of the now-
famous spiral tunnels under Field Hill to
reduce the length of switchback line that
had to be travelled. Essentially, zigzag
sections up and down mountains, and
switchbacks, reduced the grade that trains
had to negotiate by the addition of distance
through the incorporation of long loops at

There are many causes of railroad disasters, but two of the most common are the failure of the track and/or associated switch points, and the movement of the train at a speed too high for it to negotiate a curve. The small radius of the curve, in this illustration of a derailment, reveals how necessary it is that particular care be taken when driving the locomotive.

The geography of the American West offers the possibilities of stunning scenic views, as suggested by this photograph taken from an observation cupola of a train of the Denver & Rio Grande Western Railroad. This is the Colorado river valley near New Castle.

The four-tiered 780-ft (240-m) long railroad trestle built by Union engineers at Whiteside, Tennessee, with guard camp. This photograph was taken in 1864.

The Wendell Bollman truss bridge crossing the Monorgahela river near Fairmont, West Virginia. The bridge was first a single track, then became a double-track structure in 1912. It carried traffic from 1852 until the 1930s.

the ends of straight sections, and were a pioneering answer to the difficulties of taking railroads up hills and mountains. The Field Hill tunnels moved the switchback concept into the mountain: one tunnel is 3,206-ft (977-m) long and turns through 234 degrees, and is followed by another tunnel 2,890-ft (881-m) long and turning through 232 degrees; together they yield a height change of 93ft (28m).

The second stage of the improvement programme was the 1916 completion of the 5-mile (8-km) Connaught Tunnel. This removed turns totalling more than six full circles, as well as 5 miles of snowsheds, and lowered the maximum height of the line by 540ft (165m). Even so, this improvement still left a number of heavy grades to be worked, but the task was eased by the introduction of diesel power

and with it the opportunity for multiple operation. In the 1970s there were predictions of a possible 60 per cent increase in traffic along this line by the 1980s, and as a result CP Rail began to plan a third stage of grade-reduction improvement involving 21 miles (34km) of line in the Rogers Pass section, this including a 9-mile (14.5-km) tunnel, the longest in the North American continent.

*The highly spectacular
Lethbridge Viaduct, under
construction in Alberta,
Canada.*

In the first days of North American railroad construction, the steps that followed the completion of route planning and surveying were the creation of plans, the obtaining of rights of way, and the preparation of the programme's elements for tendering by the host of sub-contractors generally used.

The first practical task that was undertaken as the physical work on building a railroad began, was the grading of the trackway, and under ideal conditions there was a nice balance to be struck between cutting and filling so that material removed to make a cutting through a hill could be employed to fill in the creation of a nearby embankment. Culverts were constructed through the base of any embankment to provide free passage of any watercourses, and on level ground, ditches were dug on each side of the trackway to keep the roadbed above the surface, improving drainage and reducing the chances of snow blocking the track.

Once the trackway and associated roadbed had been created, the next task was the placing of the cross ties which supported the rails. In early days, various ideas that were tried included piles sunk in the ground and stone sills laid along the surface, but wooden ties were soon accepted as the best method. As techniques improved, it became customary to undertake a chemical treatment of the wooden ties to extend their lives, usually with the pressure application of very hot creosote. A system of steel ties was

developed by the Carnegie steel company, and used for a time on the Bessemer & Lake Erie Railroad early in the 20th century, and later in the same century concrete ties received considerable approval, although these are still very much in the minority in North America.

Once the ties had been placed, the rails were laid. Initially iron rails, weighing just 30lb (13.7kg) per yard, were standard, but over the years the weight and thus the strength and durability of the rail were increased, and from the 1870s rails of rolled steel began to become standard. Current rails weigh 132lb (60kg) per yard, and weights of up to 155lb (70kg) per yard have been used on some railroads. At first, each rail was attached to its ties with just four spikes, but as the weight of trains increased the number of spikes was increased to provide greater support. In more recent times, welded rail has come to be seen as ideal, the gaps that previously occurred every 13 yards (12m) being eliminated to provide a smoother high-speed ride; but welded rail is generally used only on the busiest lines.

Modern technology has also allowed the extensive automation of the tracklaying process. Machinery is employed to lift the old rails and remove the old ties, insert new ties and pack new ballast around them. Such operations are costly, as indicated by the fact that in 1977 the Rock Island Railroad spent $5 million on the upgrading of 134 miles (216km) of double-track line between Joliet and Rock Island. The line had been allowed to

LEFT
A train on one of the Bollman truss bridges on the Maryland North Branch of the Baltimore & Ohio Railroad. The train ran between Baltimore and Wheeling and back, carrying 40 artists & photographers, who made frequent stops so that they could take photographs and paint the scene.

BELOW LEFT
The bridge at Canyon Diabolo in Arizona on the Atchison, Topeka & Santa Fe.

Using radio communication, an engineer on the Santa Fe Railroad supervises the unloading of quarter-mile sections of welded rail from flatcars.

deteriorate since the 1950s as a consequence of falling revenues, themselves stemming from the combination of declining traffic and increasing competition for the surviving traffic; but in the longer term the knock-on effects of this deterioration were seen as counter-productive in factors such as reduced permissible speeds and lessened operating efficiency, resulting in a further loss of business.

Before specialized machinery became readily available, the laying of new track required the use of great manpower. Even so, careful and skilled organization allowed extraordinary results to be achieved: between April and October 1887, for example, the St. Paul, Minneapolis & Manitoba Railroad extended its system through Dakota and Montana by no less than 545 miles (877km) with the aid of a 10,000-man workforce. Considerable work then had to be completed before the road was fully finished, but the line was already generating revenue even as these final stages were being completed. Some 20 years later the Milwaukee Road was built across 2,300 miles (3700km) of Montana, Idaho and Washington states to Seattle in just three years.

Laying of the track is only the first stage in the line's life, of course, for laid track needs a steady diet of maintenance including, under ideal conditions, a twice-daily visual inspection of busy sections for early discovery of misalignment or other such faults. One of the main reasons for the Pennsylvania Railroad's position of

Union Pacific's EMD DD35 5,000-hp No. 75 diesel locomotive pulls a mixed freight train, including piggyback containers, past a trackside maintenance gang busy re-laying track and sleepers at Neals, Utah.

superiority toward the end of the 19th century was the importance it attached to track maintenance, supplemented by an annual inspection of the whole road.

Even though every effort was made in laying out any railroad to keep the track as straight and flat as possible, the construction of railroads inevitably required the building of bridges to carry the railroad safely over rivers, gorges, narrow valleys and similar depressions too deep for the use of embankments. And as with other aspects of railroad construction, the North Americans soon developed a distinctive type of bridge dissimilar from that of the Europeans on the other side of the Atlantic.

Stone-arched bridges, commonly found in Europe, were also built for North American railroads in regions in which stone was readily available and durability was considered important. The approach to the Harlem valley bridge, for example, was supported on stone spans of 60ft (18.3m), and the lines to and from the depot of the Pennsylvania Railroad in Philadelphia were carried by a series of brick arches, each of which spanned one street.

The vast numbers and sizes of the rivers and other gaps that had to be crossed as the railroads spread from areas of high population density, together with the problems with the availability of high-grade stone and the skilled masons required for the construction of such structures, made them impractical for the vast majority of bridging requirements. In

the early days of railroad expansion, the most attractive alternative to stone was wood. Thus the wooden trestle bridge became standard all over North America. As it expanded across Maryland, the Baltimore & Ohio Railroad reached Harper's Ferry in 1834 but had to wait for two years before a bridge became available to its further progress. An odd feature of this bridge was the fact that it incorporated a junction with the branch line to Washington in its centre, above the river; but the frequency of floods that destroyed the bridge soon persuaded the railroad to alter its arrangement, a metal bridge replacing the wooden unit during 1852.

Seasoned timber at least two years old was the ideal material for safe construction, but as the railroads fanned out into the hinterland of the North American continent the construction teams were faced with a dilemma as the speed of their advance meant that seasoned timber was not available locally and they often used fresh wood, which is horribly prone to shrinking and warping as it dries. The solution that was found for the overcoming of this problem was the Howe truss, which incorporated adjustment screws in the joints, allowing compensation to be made for the timber's shrinkage and warping.

The obvious advantage of the timber trestle type of bridge was that it opened the way for construction by unskilled workmen using locally available materials and simple tools, so for the early period of

railroad expansion it was very much the norm for railroad purposes. The use of timber trestle bridges raised problems of its own, however, for this type of structure demanded frequent inspection and maintenance, and the timbers needed regular replacement for continued structural integrity in the face of unseasoned timber's short life before the onset of rot. As a result, wood was replaced by iron as the primary structural medium for bridge-building from the 1870s. Even so, it was the timber bridges that allowed the huge expansion of the North American railroad system between the 1830s and the 1870s, and there were some very large wooden trestle bridges. By far the longest of them was the 20-mile (32-km) trestle bridge completed in 1904 across the Great Salt Lake as part of the Lucin cut-off on the Southern Pacific Railroad's cut-off of the original Promontory route. This wooden trestle bridge was gradually supplanted by an embankment created by earth tipped over the sides in a fashion that was used for the replacement of many other such bridges.

Shorter by a very considerable degree, but very much more imposing in visual terms, was the Great Trestle on the Colorado Midland Railroad's line in the Rocky Mountains. This was more than 1,000-ft (305-m) long and was part of a great system of loops by which the track reached the Ivanhoe Pass, and carried the line on a curve. The Great Trestle was abandoned in 1900.

Timber was also employed for the

American navvies at work at Roseby's Rock, linking Baltimore to Ohio on the Baltimore & Ohio Railroad. 24 December 1852.

construction of snowsheds on stretches of railroad running through mountain areas. These snowsheds were built to prevent the line from being blocked by heavy snowfalls and also to protect them from destruction by avalanches. These twin problems were of considerable magnitude: a single snow slide could often involve 100,000 tons of snow. Snowsheds were thus a genuinely vital part of railroad construction: the Central Pacific Railroad once had 60 miles (97km) of snowsheds in service to protect its line across the Sierra Nevada in the eastern part of California.

The basic feature of the majority of bridges was the truss, in structural terms a girder created by a framework of individual members. At first, trusses were built up of plates in the form of a box, as employed by Robert Stephenson, the great British engineer, in the classic Victoria bridge over the St. Lawrence river at Montreal: bridges of this type were extremely strong, but required a very high level of maintenance. On the whole, therefore, American bridge builders preferred the suspension bridge with its reduced material and maintenance requirements. A classic and early example of the suspension bridge in North American railroad service was the Niagara Falls bridge, which was completed in 1855. In general, the flexibility of suspension bridges, a problem overcome in the Niagara Falls bridge by making the span as two floors trussed together, meant that suspension bridges were not in fact designed or built as extensively for railroad service as might at first have seemed likely.

For reasons of economy, metal pins in pre-formed holes were preferred to rivets in the construction of iron bridges, and the crossing of wide gaps was achieved by the use of a series of end-to-end trusses whose junctions were supported by masonry or metal-truss piers. The piers, with their foundations made from massive wooden piles driven into the river bed, or masonry worked inside a coffer dam from which the water had been pumped, often had as much if not more of their overall length below the water as above it. During the late 1890s, the engineers of the Illinois Central Railroad built a bridge over the Ohio river at Cairo and had to allow 60ft (18.3m) between the river's high- and low-water points. The bridge built over the Mississippi river at St. Louis was based on piers whose underwater length was twice that of their height above the water.

In the absence of piers to provide support part-way along a bridge's full length, the greater length of the unsupported span requires greater depth in the truss. The extreme example of this is the Metropolis bridge over the Ohio river at Paducah in Kentucky: built by the engineers of the Burlington Northern Railroad, this bridge has a span of 720ft (219m) with a truss height of 110ft (33.5m). The other side of the coin is the fact that where numerous piers can be provided, there is no practical limit to the length of the bridge that can be built with end-to-end spans: the Huey P. Long bridge of the

Southern Pacific Railroad over the Mississippi river at New Orleans in Louisiana measures 4.4 miles (7.1km) in length and the longest single span is 790ft (241m).

When, for any of several reasons, it is impossible to build adequate piers for a suspension bridge, the engineer had recourse to a cantilever bridge as one of his most favoured alternatives. This type of structure is based on the use of self-supporting elements built out from the ends to support a smaller girder structure in the centre. Cantilevers are employed for the biggest river crossings, and the longest-span railroad bridge of all, the Quebec bridge of the Canadian National Railway Company over the St. Lawrence river, is such a one. A design fault caused one of the incomplete cantilevers to collapse in 1907, and after work had been restarted during 1910, the central span was dropped in the river during the first attempt to put it into position in 1916, before being finally fixed in 1917. Other notable cantilever bridges in Canada include the Lachine bridge over the St. Lawrence river at Montreal and the bridge at Niagara.

The first cantilever railroad bridge to be built in North America, however, was that over the Kentucky river at Cincinnati in Ohio. Here a canyon 1,200ft (366m) in width and 275ft (84m) in depth carries water whose levels could change by as much as 55ft (16.75m). To allow the railroad to cross this obstacle, the engineers started with a pair of 177-ft (54-

m) iron piers on masonry foundations in the river, and then added three 375-ft (114-m) cantilever spans to bridge the gaps between the banks and the piers at a height of about 275ft (84m) above the bottom of the river.

The current state of the bridge-builder's science is based on the ready availability of steel and concrete as his primary structural materials. This had permitted the design and construction of great arched bridges. An early example was the St. Louis bridge over the Mississippi river, where the need to avoid the use of piers was dictated by areas of quicksand in the river bed and the frequent presence on the surface of the water of ice floes and debris.

OPPOSITE

A continuous length of welded rail is threaded into the centre of existing fish-plated track during welded laying operations on the Santa Fe Railroad.

BELOW

During mechanized welded rail-laying operations on the Santa Fe Railroad, hydraulic spike pullers were used in the replacing of track.

CHAPTER SIX
CANADIAN BEGINNINGS

RIGHT

The huge size and relatively small population of Canada make it inevitable that Canadian railroads traverse large areas of country interspersed with only small townships.

The large-scale development of railways in Canada was slow to get under way, largely as a result of the country's low population density and the availability of alternatives such as water transport. Even so, it was in 1832 that the first Canadian railway was chartered. Established between the Richelieu river at St. John and La Prairie, across the St. Lawrence river from Montreal, the Champlain & St. Lawrence Railrway was just over 14-miles (22.5-km) long and cut 90 miles (145km) from the river route, linking Lake Champlain and Montreal that was currently the main line of communication between the New England states of the U.S.A. and the main city of Lower Canada. Services began on 21 July 1836, when a Stephenson Samson-type locomotive took an hour each way to haul two coaches on a round trip beginning and ending at La Prairie. In its first years of operation, the Champlain & St. Lawrence Railway halted its service when the rivers froze in winter, preventing the movement of the boats with whose operations the

railway's services were linked, and started a schedule of services right through the year only in 1851, when an extension was completed to Rouses Point, in New York state, to provide a connection with American lines and so give passengers the ability to travel by rail right through to Boston and New England.

Other early Canadian railways were built to bridge gaps in the river and lake transport systems that were still Canada's most useful lines of communication. As may be imagined from their nature, these linking railways were generally short; the first of them was the Montreal & Lachine Railway that began services in November 1848 between Montreal and the head of the Lachine rapids, the starting point of the river route to the west. In 1850 a railway was built to link the small town of Industrie, now called Joliette, with the St. Lawrence River. The 12^1/2-mile (20-km) Carillon & Grenville Railway was built round a stretch of rapids on the Ottawa river in 1854, and during the next year the

190

Locomotive No. 66, the first locomotive to be turned out of Intercolonial Railway's Moncton shops in 1876.

Northern Railway was completed to provide a link between Toronto on Lake Ontario and Collingwood on the Georgian Bay of Lake Huron.

A comparatively large number of other short railways were created during the 19th century and served their various communities and the travelling public

well. There were also ambitious plans during the same basic period for longer railways, but these often foundered on the problems of obtaining official permission from the different administrations of the separate colonies of what at the time was British North America. Some of these schemes were realized to the extent of

small but nonetheless useful segments within the context of the larger routes that had been or indeed were still being planned. Typical of these was the railway linking Halifax and Truro in Nova Scotia, which was brought into service during 1853. By far the most significant of these routes, however, was the railway linking

LEFT
A passenger train pauses in front of the Toronto, Hamilton & Buffalo Railway station and offices at Hamilton, Ontario.

BELOW LEFT
The original Stony Creek Bridge in British Columbia.

BELOW RIGHT
An old Grand Trunk station at St. Williams, Ontario.

Longeuil, opposite Montreal on the St. Lawrence river, with Portland on the coast of the American state of Maine: the Canadian section, more formally known as the St. Lawrence & Atlantic Railroad, combined with the Atlantic & St. Lawrence Railroad of the U.S.A. during 1853 to provide a rail service between Montreal and the sea, even when the Canadian city's natural access to the sea, the St. Lawrence river, was frozen in the winter. The creation of this link is also of importance as the plans for its construction led to the 1849 Guarantee Act, under whose terms the government of Canada began to provide financial assistance in the construction of railways. A new line that gained an immediate benefit from the new law's provisions was the Great Western Railway, which was completed in 1856 and provided a link between Niagara Falls, with its suspension bridge connection to Buffalo, and both Toronto and Windsor,

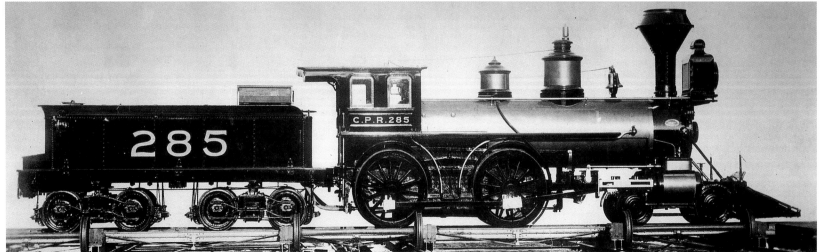

where another bridge linked the Canadian city with Detroit.

Other funding for the construction of railways in Canada came from the mother country, where British companies saw profit in the further improvement of communications within Canada. During 1852 the Canadian government approved the plans for a British company to build the Grand Trunk Railway, and by 1860 this great railway, with its celebrated Victoria Bridge at Montreal providing a link with the St. Lawrence & Atlantic Railroad and a new line to Rivière du Loup, extended westward to Sarnia, via Toronto and Stratford, on Canadian soil and from Port Huron to Detroit on U.S. territory. A 999-year lease of the Atlantic & St. Lawrence

Railroad allowed the further extension of the Grand Trunk Railway to Portland in Maine. Unfortunately, however, the establishment of this important and impressive 800-mile (1285-km) unified route between the Great Lakes and the coast of the Atlantic Ocean had unfortunate longer-term implications.

In 1845 there was established a Royal Commission on railways, and one of its tasks was to undertake the establishment of a standard gauge. This demand showed a considerable degree of foresight, especially when one thinks of the railroad chaos that had developed in other countries as a result of their failure to fix one gauge to cover the whole country. However, the commission fixed on an

RIGHT
American Standard's heyday: Grand Trunk Railway's No. 255 4-4-0.

BELOW RIGHT
The George Stephenson *locomotive, built at Hamilton for the Great Western Railway of Canada.*

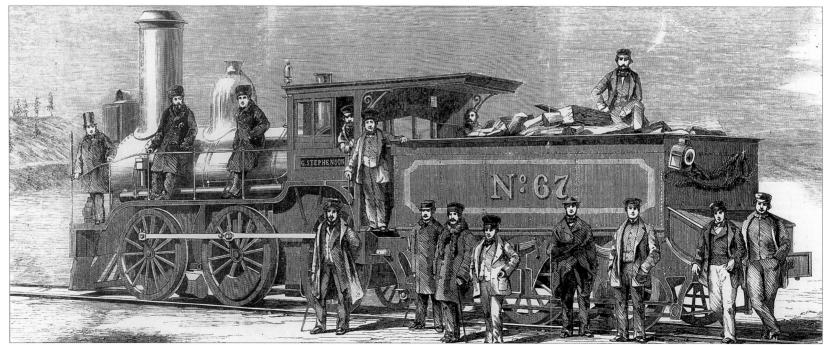

Interior of a Colonial sleeping-car of the Canadian Pacific Railway.

RIGHT

Canadian National SD40s 5131 and 5003 in the Fraser river canyon, just south of Cross-Over bridge at Cisco, British Columbia.

OPPOSITE

An eastbound Canadian National mixed freight train of 108 bogies, plus caboose, crosses Fraser River Canyon at Cisco, hauled by SD40 locomotives 5148 and 5145. The bridge in the foreground is one of Canadian Pacific Railway's.

RIGHT
Plush coach accommodation before the turn of the 19th century.

FAR RIGHT
The first trans-Canadian train on its arrival at Port Arthur on 30 June 1886.

BELOW RIGHT
Arrival of the first train into Vancouver, British Columbia, 23 May 1887.

RIGHT
Plush coach accommodation before the turn of the 19th century.

FAR RIGHT
The first trans-Canadian train on its arrival at Port Arthur on 30 June 1886.

BELOW RIGHT
Arrival of the first train into Vancouver, British Columbia, 23 May 1887.

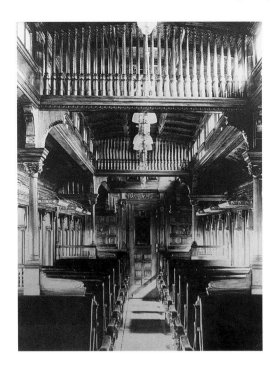

unfortunate gauge. This was the 66-in (1.68-m) gauge as currently used by the St. Lawrence & Atlantic Railroad. All Canadian railways more than 75-miles (121-km) long, including the Grand Trunk and the Great Western Railways, of which the latter had planned to use the 56.5-in (1.435-m) standard gauge so that it could attract traffic from across the border from the standard-gauge American railroad systems via its interchange facilities at Detroit and Buffalo, had to adopt a gauge that had been created with provincial rather than national demands in mind. The new Canadian national gauge remained standard for some 20 years.

The next major Canadian rail system was the Intercolonial Railway, which was

the trunk line between Halifax and Quebec that had first been suggested as early as 1832. An early problem was the 1842 resolution of the border dispute with the U.S.A. concerning the eastern frontier line between the two countries, for this located part of the railway's planned route across the northern extension of the state of Maine, delaying the creation of the Intercolonial Railway for some time.

The advisability of uniting the separate British colonies in North America acquired a measure of urgency with the outbreak of the American Civil War, especially after there emerged the possibility of the U.K. and her colonies

LEFT
A soldier stands guard beside the uncompleted new line of the Canadian Pacific Railway to the south of Moose Jaw. This line was created to provide rail services to, and more particularly from, one of the increasingly important grain-producing regions of the Canadian plains.

BELOW LEFT
In the construction of the Canadian Pacific Railway Company's line in the western part of Canada, the Canadians were faced with the same types of physical problems as the Americans, when they were driving their railroad tracks over and/or through the Rocky Mountains and their adjuncts. However, the Canadians also had to contend with smaller amounts of available finance and manpower.

OPPOSITE
Grand Trunk Pacific's locomotive No. 123 is seen while operating in support of railroad construction near Prince Rupert in British Columbia.

LEFT
Hauled by the 4-6-2 locomotive No. 196, this train in Newfoundland is running on a 3 ft 6-in (1-m) gauge track, on the only sizeable system to employ this narrow gauge anywhere in North America.

becoming involved. In October 1863 Sandford Fleming was appointed to build the railway, and completed his survey early in 1865, recommending that the line of the Intercolonial Railway extended from the northern end of the Grand Trunk Railway at Rivière du Loup along the St. Lawrence river, before turning south-west through the Matapedia valley to the Bay Chaleur and on to Moncton, where a branch from St. John joined the main line continuation to Truro and the existing railroad to Halifax. The provision of a railway connecting maritime provinces with Quebec and Ontario, as Upper and Lower Canada were now to be named, was built into the 1867 British North America Act, which created the Dominion of Canada as a confederation out of the previously separate provinces. The chief engineer was Fleming, who succeeded in developing an excellent railway.

During 1873, Prince Edward Island, which had initially refused to join

RIGHT

This is the Canadian National Railway Company's 4-8-4 locomotive No. 6167, a unit of the U2E class.

OPPOSITE

An ex-Canadian Pacific locomotive runs the Green Mountain Passenger Service at Bellows Falls, Vermont.

OPPOSITE

The Canadian Pacific Railway Company's 4-8-4 locomotive No. 1246 is now a preserved unit, operated by the Green Mountain Railroad in Vermont in the north-east of the U.S.A.

LEFT

This is another preserved steam locomotive, the Canadian Pacific Railway Company's No. 144 unit.

FAR LEFT

A feature of all North American steam locomotives that operated on the tracks running deep into the countryside between urban areas, was the addition at the front of a 'cow-catcher' device to prevent cattle and other large animals from passing under the locomotive's wheels.

CENTRE

Canadian Pacific Railway's No. 3607 2-8-0 at Toronto.

LEFT

The Toronto, Hamilton & Buffalo Railway was jointly owned by New York Central and Canadian Pacific, and as such did not own many of its own locomotives, apart from No. 45, which is shown here.

federation, largely on the grounds of the Intercolonial Railway's cost, changed its mind after seeking unsuccessfully to create its own rail system, and part of its incorporation into the Dominion of Canada had its railways taken over by the government and connected into the mainland system by train ferry.

The Intercolonial Railway was completed on 1 July 1876, but by this time a far more ambitious programme had been launched. The spurs for this larger effort were the 1869 handing over by the Hudson Bay Company of a huge area to the west of Canada proper, and the 1871 incorporation of the colony of British Columbia into the federation as the vast westernmost component of the dominion. The condition that British Columbia fixed on its accession was the construction of a railway linking the new western province

with the existing eastern provinces, with work to begin within two years and be completed within 10 years. In July 1872 Fleming set off to begin work on the route, and in the following year the detailed survey began. This took almost eight years to complete, and at times required the use of 2,000 men or more. The survey teams, and the construction parties that would eventually follow in their wake, had to contend with three basically different types of country: the wooded terrain to the west of Lake Superior, the prairies in the centre of the dominion, and the mountain ranges in the extreme west. Fleming had fixed the route by 1878 as a line that followed the northern shore of Lake Superior, headed across the prairies by way of Edmonton to the Yellowhead Pass, and finally reached Vancouver on Burrard Inlet by means of the valleys of

OPPOSITE

Railroad services hauled by steam locomotives recorded some impressive payload, speed and distance performances, but truly long-distance services hauled by the same locomotive were hampered by the need to take on more water and coal, and to dispose of ash.

LEFT

Grand Trunk Western's 4-8-4 locomotive, No. 6323, is captured by the camera at Saginaw, Wisconsin.

RIGHT

Canadian National's station at Hamilton, Ontario, optimized for functionality rather than aesthetic appeal.

BELOW

Effective control of railroad operations, as well as improving safety, was much enhanced by the introduction of electric telegraphy to link the stations of the main railroad systems. This is a railroad agent at Yananogue junction in Ontario as a fast freight train passes through his station.

OPPOSITE
BELOW RIGHT
The nature of railroad operations inevitably exerts a decisive influence on the basic layout of any station on it, but the types of internal and external decoration could be selected for local reasons. This building, photographed in about 1930, is the old Bonaventure station in Montreal.

LEFT
Seen in 1949 at the Brockville yard in Ontario, these two 4-8-4 locomotives were part of the Canadian National Railway Company's fleet. The special plate on the headlight bracket of No. 6258 indicates that it was the locomotive that hauled the train during a royal visit to Canada in 1938.

ABOVE

Sir William Cornelius Van Horne (1842–1915), first chairman and second president of the Canadian Pacific Railway Company.

ABOVE RIGHT

A view of Canadian Pacific Railway's Banff Springs Hotel, Banff, Alberta. Photographed c. 1928.

the Thompson and Fraser rivers.

In the time that the surveys were undertaken, a decision had to be reached as to who was to undertake the construction of the huge railway. In 1872 it was decided that the task should be contracted to private enterprise, and the two companies which received the necessary charters were the Interoceanic and the Canada Pacific. In 1873, however, the government of Canada resigned as a result of the political scandal stemming

from efforts to secure a merger of the two companies.

The completion of a line from Emerson, on the American border, to Winnipeg gave this central city an indirect means of railway communication with the eastern part of Canada by means of American track to Chicago, but the rest of the decade saw little progress on the transcontinental line. In 1880 a sense of urgency was added to the question, for there was some discussion south of the

border for the American annexation of Canada's central prairie region. At this stage, therefore, George Stephen was persuaded to head a team that put together a new syndicate to take over the construction of the new railway. This led to the February 1881 incorporation of the Canadian Pacific Railway Company with Stephen as its president and James J. Hill, later the father of the Great Northern Railway in the U.S.A., as a member of the board. Hill was also a comparatively early

Construction work on the Connaught Tunnel on the Canadian Pacific Railway.

RIGHT
The eastbound Canadian National passing through the foothills of the Rockies after negotiating roughly 100 miles (160km) of Montana since leaving Vancouver.

OPPOSITE
Multiple heading allows the Canadian Pacific Railway to haul enormous freight trains, a system that promotes efficiency and boosts operating revenues.

departure as he left over the decision to follow the route north of Lake Superior rather than build via Sault Ste.-Marie and across the northern end of the U.S.A. Even so, the contribution of Hill to the Canadian Pacific Railway before he left was very considerable, not least in his pressure to employ William Van Horne as the company's general manager.

Horne had earlier worked for the Illinois Central and the Chicago, Milwaukee & St. Paul Railroads, and left the latter at the beginning of 1882 to join the Canadian Pacific Railway. With Stephen, who had earlier been the president of the Bank of Montreal, looking

after the company's financial affairs and Van Horne overseeing the more practical aspects of the company's operations, work on the construction of the new railway finally began in earnest during 1882. A government grant of $25 million and 25 million acres (10000000 hectares) of land, as well as the short sections of track that were already in existence, were the starting points for the Canadian Pacific Railway. Progress with the creation of the track presented enormous physical difficulties, especially in the crossing of the Rocky Mountains and, perhaps even worse, the traverse around the north of Lake Superior through a horrendous mix

of swamp and rock. Even so, progress was made, and the track reached Calgary during August 1883.

One of the main reasons that the survey of the potential routes for the Canadian Pacific Railway had opted for a more southerly route had been the fear that American railroads, then extending rapidly over the north-western parts of the U.S.A., might siphon off Canadian traffic if the route was fixed along a more northern line. This meant that the line had to cross the Rocky Mountains between Calgary and Vancouver by means of Kicking Horse Pass, which meant that the track had to progress along gradients as steep as 4.4

Stony Creek Bridge in the Rocky Mountains, 1878.

Continental Limited *of the Canadian National Railways, crossing the Fraser river at Cisco, British Columbia. The Canadian Pacific main line is in the right foreground. At Cisco the CNR and the CPR, which had followed the left and right banks respectively of the Thompson and Fraser rivers, changed over to the opposite banks for the remaining 150 miles (240km) to Vancouver.*

RIGHT
Richmond Station, Quebec, in 1930.

OPPOSITE
One of an order of 29 new locomotives being loaded at Montreal in late 1956 for rail services in Newfoundland.

OPPOSITE
LEFT
Canadian Pacific Railway's snowplough No. 2 in a Sierra snowshed in the 1870s.

OPPOSITE RIGHT and LEFT
Canadian National Railway No. 5293 at Sherbrooke, PQ, waiting to take a night train back to Montreal on a snowy Saturday night. The photographs epitomize the railway scene in the last years of steam and reflect the wonderful dry cold of a Canadian winter. These 4-6-2s were used on local services over most of the Canadian National system.

OPPOSITE
The eastbound Canadian National, in the Rockies between Banff and Calgary.

LEFT
While the eastbound Canadian National train was held at a signal to allow a westbound freight to arrive and enter a passing loop, it was caught up by a following freight, 15 miles (24km) east of Banff.

Two SD40-2 locomotives, Nos. 5913 and 5847, haul a Canadian Pacific eastbound freight train of 80 bogies along the Thompson river canyon, just north of Lyton, British Columbia.

The old and new are seen together as locomotive No. 6218 pulls out of a Canadian station, beneath the electric power lines of a newer generation of engines.

per cent. Continued problems along the Lake Superior and mountain sections then coincided with a shortage of adequate funding to delay work on the Canadian Pacific Railway until, in 1885, the government of Canada agreed to lend the Canadian Pacific Railway the required resources after the importance of the operation had been confirmed by the use of completed sections of track to ferry troops for the suppression of a rebellion in the area of Winnipeg.

The injection of new resources allowed the completion of the Canadian Pacific Railway on 8 November 1885, and by June 1886 the first scheduled through trains were operating between Montreal and Port Moody. The latter was just a short distance from Vancouver, and this last section was completed in 1887.

The creation of this first Canadian railway across the continent to the Pacific Ocean spurred a rush of further development in the Canadian railway system, with the Canadian Pacific Railway itself to the fore. One area that was to profit from this process was at the eastern end of the Canadian Pacific Railway's route where, because of rivalry between Montreal and Toronto, the government of Canada had fixed a 'non-aligned' eastern terminus at the eastern end of Lake Nipissing. The Canadian Pacific Railway which was already the owner of an existing line along the Ottawa valley to provide it with a link to Montreal, soon bought a miscellany of other small railways to allow it to spread its schedule

OPPOSITE
FAR LEFT
An H-5-class subway train near Eglinton station, Toronto.

ABOVE RIGHT
Toronto, Hamilton & Buffalo Railway diesel-electric locomotive No. 75 and freight train, photographed at an unknown location.

BELOW RIGHT
A locomotive of Ontario Northland Railway.

LEFT
ABOVE
Engine No. 204 in the Dunvegan yards of Northern Alberta Railway.

BELOW
An Ontario Northlander.

OPPOSITE
LEFT
A Canadian National freight train carrying iron ore over a trestle bridge at South river, Ontario.

RIGHT
Canadian National freight train passing track expansion works east of Jasper.

LEFT
A Canadian National freight train in Quebec.

OPPOSITE
Railroad communications are of especial significance in a large country such as Canada, with vast quantities of raw materials and a small population typified by urban and industrial centres often very distant from each other.

LEFT
In mountainous regions, of which Canada has a high proportion, the valleys carved out of the rock by rivers often provide an excellent starting point for the creation of railroad services. This is part of the Canadian Pacific Railway Company's route along the valley of the Thomson river.

OPPOSITE
A passenger service of the Quebec, North Shore & Labrador Railway passes through the Sept-Îles area.

LEFT
This is a triple-headed freight service of the Cartier Railway, which hauls iron ore between Lac Jeannine and Port Cartier.

Preserved at Canada's National Museum of Science and Technology outside Ottawa, the 4-8-4 locomotive No. 6200 was a U2G-class unit of the Canadian National Railway Company.

RIGHT
Canadian Pacific Railway 4-4-4 locomotive No. 2928.

BELOW RIGHT
Canadian Pacific Railway 4-6-2 No. 2469 in Toronto.

OPPOSITE
The nature of the Canadian long-distance railroad network, as the country developed in the second half of the 19th century and first quarter of the 20th century, placed particular emphasis on passenger operations, and on power in combination with high water and fuel capacities for the greatest possible speed and range. This was also combined with good engineering to ensure the maximum possible reliability, and a not inconsiderable number of locomotives. This includes No. 1278 of the Canadian Pacific Railway Company, which has survived to become a cherished museum piece.

RIGHT

The development of the railroad system in Canada, after it had secured its initial viability, was often dictated by the commercial need to exploit the magnificent scenery that was sometimes located only a comparatively short distance from an urban location. This is an observation area overlooking the Algoma Central Railway.

to Toronto and Quebec, and created a branch to Sault Ste.-Marie in 1888. This programme of line extensions was undertaken within the context of traffic agreements the Canadian Pacific Railway had reached with the Minneapolis & St. Paul and the Duluth, South Shore & Atlantic Railroads as protection against the increasing commercial threat represented by the growing northern railroad being created by James Hill. In the region to the east of the St. Lawrence river, the Canadian Pacific Railway's system was pushed forward in 1889 to St. John in the province of New Brunswick by means of the direct route across the American state of Maine. This route was created from an extension of the South Eastern Railway to Mattawamkeag, and a junction with the Maine Central Railroad. In the following year the Canadian Pacific Railway completed its transcontinental route by leasing the New Brunswick Railway system as the last link in its service to St. John.

William McKenzie and Donald Mann, who had earlier worked for the Canadian Pacific Railway, began in the 1890s to develop their own railway system. In 1896 the two men began to build the Lake Manitoba Railway up the western side of the eponymous lake, and then extended this to Winnipegosis with the help of federal land grants and financial assistance from the provincial government. In 1899 the name of the Lake Manitoba Railway was changed to the Canadian Northern Railway, and this operator grew steadily as

Canadian Pacific Hudson-type 4-6-4 No. 2842, leaving Windsor station, Montreal, in 1938.

CANADIAN BEGINNINGS

Where freight hauling was the primary task that the locomotive designer had to build into his design, aesthetic appearance could be sacrificed to utilitarianism. This was certainly the case with the Canadian Pacific Railway Company's locomotive No. 2815.

a result of a programme of takeover and construction supervised by McKenzie and Mann: the system developed links to Winnipeg and the border between Canada and the U.S.A., and Port Arthur on the shore of Lake Superior. The two men proceeded with financial prudence to enlarge the Canadian Northern Railway by this system of cost-effective construction, where required, and purchase where there was existing track, and by 1905 the Canadian Northern Railway system extended from Edmonton in the western province of Alberta to Lake Superior in the east, with other small sections around Montreal and Quebec. By the first decade of the 20th century, Mackenzie and Mann were ready to develop their own

Canadian Pacific train No. 4 climbs eastward in Kicking Horse Pass above the Upper Spiral Tunnel, headed by an S2a-class locomotive 5813 and a Tlb-class 5929. 1947.

transcontinental railway to rival that of the Canadian Pacific Railway. Over a period of some seven years, therefore, the Canadian Northern Railway was expanded to the west toward the Pacific Ocean along a line established by Fleming through Yellowhead Pass to Vancouver, and to the east in a long curve well clear of the northern side of Lake Superior to reach Sudbury and Toronto. By 1916, therefore, the Canadian Northern Railway was able to start scheduled services linking Quebec and Vancouver, while the inauguration of an electrified system through a tunnel under Mount Royal permitted services to a new terminus in Montreal and thence to an eastward extension of the system into Nova Scotia.

Over this period the Grand Trunk Railway had concentrated its efforts on developing its own network in Canada, while at the same time enhancing its connections with the railroads of the north-eastern part of the U.S.A. The 1897 opening of a new bridge at Niagara Falls and the addition of a new steel superstructure to the Victoria Bridge allowed the carriage of traffic swelled by the Grand Trunk's acquisition of the Central Vermont Railway to the Connecticut coastal city of New London. The prudence with which the Grand Trunk Railway expanded did not match that of the Great Northern Railway and, finding itself somewhat overextended financially, the Grand Trunk secured the services of Charles Hayes, lately of the Wabash Railroad. Hayes' new financial broom and his linking of the Grand Trunk Railway's services with those of the Wabash Railroad soon swept the Grand Trunk Railway's balance sheet to a more healthy state.

By this time, in the early years of the 20th century, Canada was receiving larger numbers of immigrants and its national economy was growing comparatively quickly, so Hayes believed that the creation of a third transcontinental railway was financially feasible. This new operator was the Grand Trunk Pacific, created specifically for the task. During 1903 the Grand Trunk Pacific secured an agreement with the government of Canada for the establishment of a National Transcontinental Railway. The agreement

OPPOSITE
This triple-headed freight service of the Canadian Pacific Railway Company is caught by the camera in the Revelstoke area of British Columbia.

LEFT
This service, hauled by locomotive No. 6542, is a Canadian National Railway Company passenger operation in the Ottawa region.

249

RIGHT
Work on the Quebec, North Shore & Labrador Railway started in 1950 with the object of providing a means to transport iron ore from Sept-Îles to Schefferville.

OPPOSITE
Seen in the form of one of its services just outside the port area of Halifax, Nova Scotia, VIA Rail was established by the Canadian federal government during the 1960s to undertake passenger operations deemed essential to the commercial and social development of Canada.

was based on the construction, by the government, of a line stretching from Moncton in the province of New Brunswick right across the provinces of Quebec and Ontario to Winnipeg, capital of the province of Manitoba. Once complete, this line was to be leased to the Grand Trunk Pacific, which was to undertake the construction of a line from Winnipeg to the Pacific coast in British Columbia.

The government's eastern portion of the new route was planned to very exacting standards with an eye to the minimum possible gradients, and was directed through regions that were largely unsurveyed and only vestigially populated. The Grand Trunk Pacific's western portion, on the other hand, was often little more than a parallel partner to the existing lines of the Canadian Pacific and Canadian Northern Railway's western

sections. One of the primary financial concepts behind the planning of the new railway was the possibility of attracting the grain traffic from Canada's water and lake routes on its way to the ports of the Atlantic seaboard for shipment to Europe. For this reason, the first portion of the new railway was constructed from Port Arthur, at the head of Lake Superior, and the launch of grain-delivery services to the port during 1910. At the other end of the

CANADIAN BEGINNINGS

Two rebuilt GP9s and a rebuilt GP7 push the last two boxcars over the hump at Canadian Pacific's Toronto yard. Entrance to the yard is in the centre background with the main Toronto to Montreal lines.

The Canadian Pacific Railway Company's operations extend into the U.S.A., as indicated by this photograph of a CP freight service at Dayton's Bluff near St. Paul on the Missouri river.

new transcontinental line, the Grand Trunk Pacific ignored the well established port and railway centre around Puget Sound and instead fixed its western end at Prince Rupert, a new port that was to be created on the estuary of the Skeena river near Port Simpson, some 550 miles (885km) to the north of Vancouver.

One notable advantage offered by the new railway was the fact that it avoided both the Kicking Horse Pass route and the muskeg (region of mixed water/partially dead vegetation bog, often covered by a layer of sphagnum or other mosses) around Lake Superior: both of these had been major obstacles for the Canadian Pacific

Railway. Using a workforce of 25,000 men and large quantities of equipment and supplies brought into Prince Rupert by ship, the western section of the Grand Trunk Pacific had been completed by April 1914, and in the following year the new National Transcontinental Railway line to the east was completed.

The Grand Trunk Railway, whose contract to operate the government-built eastern end of the National Transcontinental Railway demanded an annual rental of 3 per cent of the construction cost, feared for its financial survival as the construction cost had been $150 million, three times the budgeted figure. Moreover, the fact that World War I was being bitterly fought in Europe had dried the flow of immigrants and also of investment to Canada. The Grand Trunk Railway therefore decided that the successful operation of the complete National Transcontinental Railway, over both its own western and government-built eastern sections, was financially impossible. At much the same time and for the same general reasons, the

ABOVE and OPPOSITE
This freight service, near Williams Lake, is double-headed by locomotives of a Canadian operator, BC (British Columbia) Rail, and an American operator, the Atchison, Topeka & Santa Fe Railroad.

RIGHT and OPPOSITE
*As indicated by its name,
which was originally British
Columbia Railway, BC Rail
operates services in British
Columbia. This is the
westernmost part of Canada,
with the Rocky Mountains
passing through its eastern
regions, and offers superb
scenery for rail travellers,
such as this area of Lillooet.*

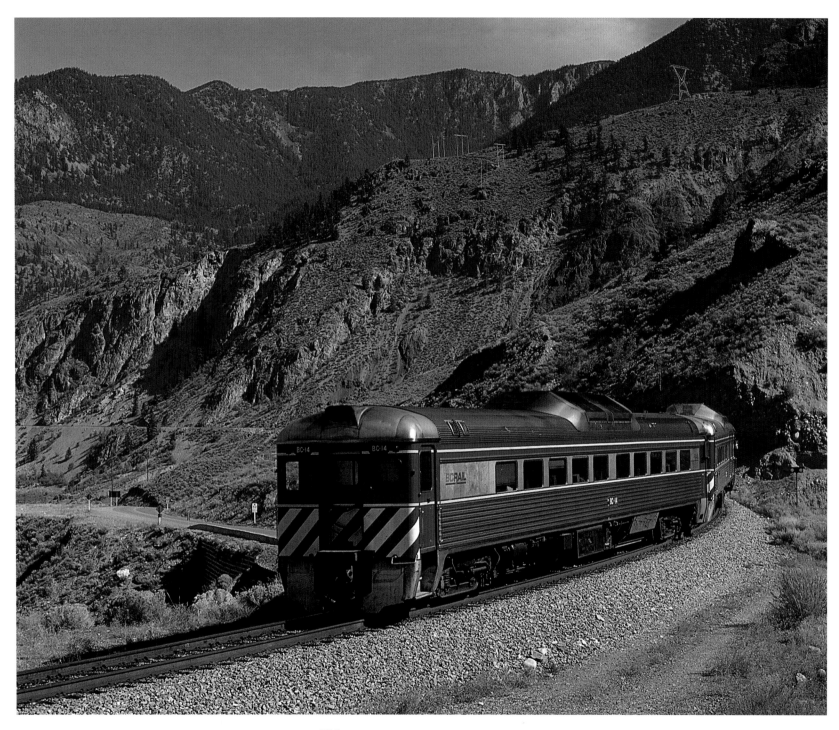

RIGHT
View of the Canadian Pacific Calgary rail yards from the tower.

OPPOSITE
Two SD40-2 locomotives Nos. 753 and 758 at the British Columbia Railway depot, North Vancouver.

Canadian Northern Railway had discovered that it could not return a profit on the operation of its own transcontinental railway.

A royal commission was established in 1916 to look into the matter of transcontinental railway operations, and subsequently recommended that the optimum way of resolving the problems was the nationalization of the Grand Trunk, Grand Trunk Pacific, and Canadian Northern Railways. The resolution of the three operators' financial situations took some time, but by 1918 it was feasible to create the Canadian National Railway Company to take over the three semi-moribund private railways. The Canadian National Railway Company initially took over the existing publicly-owned railways and also the Canadian Northern Railway, added the Grand Trunk Pacific in 1920, and absorbed the parent company in 1923.

The new board of directors was led by Sir Henry Thornton, an American who had begun his railroad career on the Pennsylvania Railroad, become general superintendent of the Long Island Rail Road and, just before his Canadian appointment, was the general manager of a classic British railway, the Great Eastern, a position he had held in World War I in parallel with two other appointments, namely chief engineer of the Great Eastern Railway and director of railway transport in France. The very highly experienced Thornton was well suited to the tricky task of knitting the disparate elements of the Canadian National Railway Company into

Integrated port and railroad facilities at Halifax in Nova Scotia ensure that pre-loaded containers are moved swiftly and reliably between container ships and the special flatcars of the Canadian railroads that move these flatcars to and from the port.

a homogeneous whole, and also rationalizing with the constituent elements' financial affairs and contractual obligations. A monumental task, Thornton was fortunate to have a free hand from the government of Canada, whose sole demand was that all outstanding commitments be honoured.

Thornton soon discovered that a large number of the lines that he now controlled needed major improvements,

but in the following 10 years achieved wonders; on his departure, Thornton left the Canadian National Railway Company a financially sound and operationally excellent system. Thornton had rationalized and also improved the network he had inherited from the constituent railway companies, and also launched the expansion of the system with the construction of lines into the Peace river area of northern Alberta and the

addition of the Long Lac cut-off between the old Canadian Northern and Grand Trunk lines, in the process trimming the distance between North Bay and Winnipeg by just over 100 miles (160km).

The Canadian Pacific Railway had passed through financial difficulties in the 1890s, but then began to fare better as immigration to Canada accelerated in the early years of the 20th century. In 1899 the Canadian Pacific Railway created a new

A Canadian National roundhouse in Toronto, with a VIA Rail twin on the turntable and a turbo train being shunted on the main line. Photographed from the CN tower.

line through Crows Nest Pass, the southern crossing over the Selkirk mountains that had originally been rejected as a route to Vancouver as it lay close to the Canadian border with the U.S.A., and this provided good access to major coal deposits in the area, which boomed and in the process boosted the profitability of the railway.

One of the most constructionally and technically significant achievements of this period in the history of the Canadian railway system was the famous spiral tunnels, completed in 1909 as a means of effecting a major reduction in the severity of the grades through Kicking Horse Pass. Another major success of the same year was the Lethbridge viaduct over the Belly river on the Crow's Nest Pass line: more than 5,000-ft (1525-m) long, the viaduct is 314ft (96m) above the water and is the highest railway bridge in Canada. Other achievements included the 5-mile (8-km) Connaught Tunnel under Mount MacDonald, the opening of which removed the need for a 450-ft (137-m) ascent to the top of Rogers Pass.

At much the same time as it was accomplishing these and other technical achievements, the Canadian Pacific Railway was also building up its network of branch lines in the prairies. In the prosperous years of the 1920s, the Canadian National Railway Company pursued the same course, and there was a vigorous level of competition. The economic depression of the 1930s, following the crash of 1929, ended this

OPPOSITE
*This is VIA Rail's locomotive
No. 6418.*

LEFT
*Tail-end driving car of
Ontario Northland
Railway's ex-Dutch TEE
trainset No. 1986, forming
'Northlander' Train 121 to
North Bay and Timmins,
just leaving Toronto.*

Moncton by only a single line, and this exerted enormous pressure on the limited capabilities of this line, which were maximized from 1941 by the introduction of a system of centralized train control.

The boom in railway transport in Canada during World War II was followed from 1945 by a steep decline in demand as the need for huge shipments to Europe declined, and the combination of improved road and air transport took their toll. To ensure their survival as viable financial bodies, the Canadian railways undertook a major effort to improve their operating efficiencies. A first step in the right direction was dieselization, or the replacement of coal-fired locomotives by diesel-engined locomotives. The Canadian railways had undertaken a number of experiments with diesel haulage in the 1930s, and after a pause during the years of World War II these developments were resumed once more. During the 1950s, therefore, both of Canada's major railway systems began the process of wholesale abandonment of coal-fired locomotion in favour of diesel-engined traction.

Another move, prompted by the need to rationalize and streamline Canadian railway operations, and thereby achieve major improvements in cost-efficiency, was the 1961 amalgamation of the Canadian Pacific Railway's U.S. subsidiaries (the Minneapolis, St. Paul & Sault Ste.-Marie, the Duluth, South Shore & Atlantic, and the Wisconsin Central Railroads) into the single Soo Line Railroad with 4,500 miles (7240km) of

OPPOSITE
Straight lines and curves. Canadian National's 32 turbo stands at Ottawa with the 11.20 hrs to Montreal.

LEFT
Rail traffic control at Edmonton, Alberta.

process and so reduced the demand for railway transport that passenger levels fell to little more than 50 per cent of their figure for 1928. So bad did the position become, moreover, that consideration was given to the merger and radical consolidation of the two major Canadian railroad systems. For a number of political as well as financial and operational reasons, though, nothing came of the concept and the two systems maintained their independence.

It was clear that something had to be done to ameliorate the situation, however, and a royal commission, established in 1931, suggested a number of ways in which the cooperation and avoidance of

duplication between the two operators could be achieved. In the event, little was done except for the sharing of passenger trains over the two systems' busiest sections, between Montreal and Toronto. Then the worst of the depression was over toward the end of the 1930s and traffic began to increase once again. World War II next demanded unprecedented levels of freight traffic, and the large scale of Canadian war production taxed Canada's railways to their limits, especially in the eastern part of the country as men, equipment, food and other items were transported to the ports of the Atlantic seaboard for shipment to the U.K. from Halifax and St. John. Halifax was fed from

track throughout the north-western part of the U.S.A. between the Great Lakes and the state of Montana.

The Canadian National Railway Company also expanded by acquisition of an overseas system in 1949, though this was not altogether removed from Canada as it was that of the island of Newfoundland, which finally became part of the Dominion of Canada. The island's railway system had been launched in the later part of the 19th century, with Sandford Fleming as its chief engineer. For reasons of cost and the island's geographical isolation, the Newfoundland Railway system was based on a gauge of

42in (1.07m). Work on the system started in 1881, but the line linking Port aux Basques with St. John's was finished only in 1898. After the Canadian National Railway Company's takeover of Newfoundland Railway in 1949, some of the island's track was converted to standard gauge.

Although in overall terms there was a slackening in demand for railway transport in Canada in the periods following World War II, there were some regions in which the demand for railway transport increased as a function of the discovery of exploitable raw materials and the need to bring in equipment and take

out the raw materials needed by Canadian industries or for export. Typical of this is the area some 350 miles (565km) north of the estuary of the St. Lawrence river around Knob Lake in a virtually uninhabited area of eastern Quebec and Labrador. Here there are vast deposits of iron ore, and in the later part of the 1940s it was estimated that it should be possible to extract some 10 million tins of ore each year if the required transport could be provided. This estimate paved the way for the start of work during 1950 on the Quebec, North Shore & Labrador Railway from Sept-Îles, on the estuary of the St. Lawrence river, to Schefferville. Work on

RIGHT

*One of the Canadian
National Railway
Company's premier
maintenance facilities is the
Atelier depot at Montreal.*

OPPOSITE

*These locomotives are lying
in wait at the Taschereau
yard in Montreal, for use by
the Canadian National
Railway Company.*

the construction of the new line was feasible only through the construction of several airstrips so that supplies could be delivered by air, but good progress was made and by 1954 ore-laden trains were running. By 1960 the addition of a branch at Carol Lake, with a length of automated track to supply the ore-crushing plant, raised the daily total of ore handled to more than 100,000 tons. To the west of this region is the Cartier Railway, which started operation in 1962 as a generally similar system connecting the iron ore deposits at Lac Jeannine and Port Cartier.

Although the primary disposition of Canada's railway lines is east/west

between the Atlantic and Pacific Coasts or points between them, there are a number of lines aligned in the north/south plane. Typical of these are the iron ore lines mentioned above, but other notable lines with this disposition include the Hudson Bay Railway, which is basically an extension of the original Canadian Northern Railway and reached Churchill on Hudson Bay in the course of 1929, and the Ontario Northland Railway to James Bay, the southern subsidiary of Hudson Bay proper. This railway was chartered by the province of Ontario during 1902 as the Temiskaming & Northern Ontario Railway, and attained James Bay in 1932.

The day of ambitious railway building in Canada was not completed by these routes in the eastern half of the country. In the west a classic example is the British Columbia Railway. The Pacific Great Eastern Railway was chartered in 1912 to build a route from Squamish through the Fraser river valley's timber country to link with the Grand Trunk Railway at Prince George. Little progress with the new line was achieved until the provincial government took control at the end of World War I, when work restarted. By 1921 344 miles (554km) had been constructed to Quesnel, but this was still some way short of the planned junction at Prince George.

Work was again halted at this point, and did not resume until 1949, when construction of the extension to Prince George was started. This was ready in 1953, and in 1956 a connecting line from Squamish to North Vancouver was added. Beyond Prince George, the line was extended farther to join the Northern Alberta Railways system at Dawson Creek, and continued north to Fort Nelson, which the line reached in 1971. At the same time, another branch was built, extending north-west to Fort St. James and thence Dease Lake. Renamed the British Columbia Railway, in April 1972 this expanding system of nearly 1,800 miles (2895km) was later taken in hand for northward extension into the Yukon Territory.

Another railway with a north/south basic alignment was established in northern Alberta. This Great Slave Lake Railway was built in 1964–65 from Roma 380 miles (612km) north to Hay River, with a branch to the lead and zinc mining area around Pine Point. The most northerly of all Canada's railways is an old-established private concern dating from the time of the Klondyke gold rush of the late 1890s. The 36-in (0.91-m) gauge White Pass and Yukon Route is 110-miles (177-km) long and was built between 1898 and 1900 from Skagway, where the prospectors landed after their sea journey to the Yukon, to Whitehorse, the capital of the Yukon Territory. The White Pass and Yukon Route lasted beyond the end of the gold boom, supported the U.S. Army in World War II, and has become very useful once more

with the opening of new mines in the Yukon Territory and the establishment of an integrated container service for transhipment of the lead/zinc concentrate by water from Skagway.

The enlargement of the Canadian railway system for the exploitation of natural resources in the remote areas of the country has been accompanied by a programme of major modernization to the main lines, as a means of improving freight services. CP Rail, as Canadian Pacific Railways was renamed in 1971 when the company was reorganized, introduced unit trains in the course of 1967, and has steadily pushed forward modern aspects of rail transport, including containerization, computer-controlled freight yards and associated computerized car-location systems, and 'piggyback' services with trailers loaded directly onto flatcars.

Passenger services went into a major decline after World War II, however. By the late 1960s passenger services were in danger of total disappearance, despite the efforts of operators such as Canadian National in matters such as the introduction of turbo-trains and refurbished 'streamliners' imported from the U.S.A. as part of a programme to offset the speed advantages offered by aircraft with the greater comfort and general passenger appeal that could be provided in modern trains. The government of Canada was mightily concerned for the continued existence of passenger services on Canada's railways, and established VIA

Rail as a federal authority to assume responsibility for passenger services. Innovation was clearly demanded, and among the new equipment introduced under VIA Rail are 125-mph (200-km/h) tilt-body LRC passenger cars for service on the route linking Montreal and Quebec, while commuter services in the Toronto area have also been improved by the introduction of diesel-powered two-level cars.

Commercially liberated from most of the expense of maintaining and operating passenger services, the two national networks are both financially stable. The Canadian National is one of the most profitable state systems in the world, and in combination with the Soo Line CP Rail has contributed more than a quarter of the parent Canadian Pacific company's net income.

OPPOSITE
Tourism is a very important aspect of their operations for most of Canada's passenger-carrying railroads, as indicated by this service with observation cars situated along its length.

CHAPTER SEVEN

LOCOMOTIVES & ROLLING STOCK

By the middle of the 19th century, the American standard type of locomotive had reached the form that was to remain almost universal for 50 years, and can therefore be accorded the unofficial but appropriate designation 'Standard' class. As noted above, the 4-4-0 wheel arrangement had been adopted at an early stage, but it was during the early part of the 1850s that Thomas Rogers of the Rogers, Ketchum & Grosvenor company of Paterson in New Jersey started to produce the locomotives introducing the definitive configuration that was then widely imitated. The most significant aspect of the concept embodied in Rogers' locomotive was a lengthened wheelbase, which permitted the horizontal mounting of the cylinders at the sides of the smokebox, which was carried on the upper part of the four-wheel pilot truck that had proved so important in providing locomotives with the ability to cope with the irregularities typical of early American track. Another standard feature, by this stage, was the equalizing beams carrying the driving wheels, while another feature of Rogers' design was the tapered boiler surrounding the large rear-set firebox.

Other external features that became typical of American locomotive manufacturing practices stemmed directly from the environment in which the locomotives were intended to operate. A large cab for the engineer and fireman was vital for the protection it provided in the enormously varied climes in which the locomotives operated; a large chimney with a spark-arrester arrangement was essential to avoid the distribution of the sparks that could readily ignite fires in the forests and prairies through which the locomotive travelled; a bell, a headlight and a cow-catcher were required to protect the train and to provide a warning of any animals on the track; and the provision of a large sandbox on top of the boiler provided the capability for the engineer to overcome the problem of slipping wheels on remote stretches of line lacking the possibility of outside aid. The Standard type was also typified by another highly visible and distinctive feature that had no practical value: this was the elaborate decoration comprising bright colours, a trim of highly polished copper and brass, and sometimes flags and/or pictures painted on the side panels. These features were all typical of the early Standard-type locomotives, and later disappeared largely because it ceased to be the practice that a crew was allocated to a particular locomotive and could therefore take a special pride in its individual machine.

So far as its internal workings were concerned, the Standard type of locomotive was based, of course, on the basic principles evolved by the British engineer George Stephenson and first wholly embodied in his famous *Rocket* locomotive of 1829. The hot gases flowing from a firebox passed through an array of tubes inside a boiler to a smokebox. The water in the boiler was heated by the passage of the hot gases through the tubes

OPPOSITE

This preserved 2-8-0 steam locomotive, No. 395 and named Whippanong, *is operated by the Morris County Central Railroad.*

LEFT

The maintenance and operation of old locomotives is an occupation for those with a deep love for such venerable objects and a keen understanding of the type of engineering that went into the design and manufacture of them.

and formed steam, which was fed into cylinders and, by acting on a piston, powered the wheels by means of a connecting rod. The rotation of the wheels was in turn transmitted to the valves admitting the steam to the cylinders, allowing the spent steam to escape from the cylinder. Finally, the exhaust steam was fed into the smokebox to create the draft required for the fire and so maintained the cycle of the complete process.

In the 1850s and 1860s the 4-4-0 Standard type of locomotive was used to haul both passenger and freight trains, of which neither could reach any great speed, but in the following decade the appearance of the Wootten firebox began to produce a change that led to generally higher performance. The Wootten firebox was designed to burn the powdery residue from anthracite coal that was otherwise wasted, and its different, wider and shallower form demanded modification of the wheel arrangement. One method that was tested was known as the camelback or Mother Hubbard: to avoid an unfortunate lengthening of the wheelbase, the engineer's cab was superimposed on the boiler, with a platform on the front of the tender so that the stoker could feed fuel into the firebox. The cab on top of the boiler had earlier been used by Ross Winans of Baltimore, and also in a locomotive series for the Baltimore & Ohio Railroad, but in both these cases the change had been effected to give the engineer a better forward field of vision.

Colorado & Southern Class E-4a 2-8-2 No. 807, built by Baldwin in 1911. The picture was taken in 1958.

RIGHT

Missouri Pacific Railroad freight, headed by Class 2100 locomotive No. 2118. 1947.

BELOW RIGHT

Santa Fe Railroad Series 2900 Northern 4-8-4 locomotive No. 2921, heading a freight train on the New Mexico Division track in the 1950s.

OPPOSITE

TOP LEFT

Union Pacific 4-6-6-4 Challenger-class locomotive No. 3827 heads a freight train east near the summit of the Cajon Pass, California, on Atchison, Topeka and Santa Fe track. A 4-10-2 and 2-8-2 push at the rear. Februrary 1947.

BELOW LEFT

H-8 No. 1655 blasts westward toward Limeville bridge on a coal train without pusher. September 1957.

TOP RIGHT

H-8 No. 1615 picking up an eastbound coal train at Quinnimont, West Virginia yards. 1949

BELOW RIGHT

A 380-class Santa Fe-type 2-10-2 locomotive built by the Baldwin Locomotive Works.

In combination with the Wootten firebox, the camelback arrangement was employed in the locomotives of several railroads, and also for locomotives of several wheel configurations.

At the time he created the firebox named for him, Wootten was the general manager of the Philadelphia & Reading Railroad, so it was perhaps inevitable that this operator should be among the primary users of this firebox. It was originally applied to 4-6-0 freight engines with small driving wheels, but for the Atlantic City route, where the Philadelphia & Reading Railroad was faced with direct competition from the Pennsylvania Railroad, Wootten developed a 2-4-2 fast passenger engine, in which the two small trailing wheels supported the firebox. As well as creating his own type of firebox, Wootten

incorporated another innovation designed by Samuel Vauclain of the Baldwin Locomotive Works. Vauclain's system of compound working was just one of several ways of using the partially expanded steam from one cylinder to work another cylinder, usually of greater diameter to allow for the extraction of the maximum possible work from the now-lowered pressure of the steam. The distinctive feature of Vauclain's system was that both cylinders drove the same cross head, thus removing some of the complications.

The 2-4-2 locomotives of the Philadelphia & Reading Railroad proved somewhat lacking in stability at the comparatively high speeds for which they were designed, and in 1896 Wootten produced a much more significant design using the 4-4-2 wheel arrangement that has become known, from its design origins and initial operational use along the eastern seaboard of the U.S.A., as the Atlantic type. The new engines proved capable of covering the 55 miles (88.5km) between Camden and Atlantic City in one hour, and in special circumstances of attaining an average speed of 71.6mph (115.25km/h).

The Pennsylvania Railroad also adopted the Atlantic type of locomotive for its competing services. The Atlantic-type locomotives of the Pennsylvania Railroad reached the peak of their development in the E6-class, of which the first example was completed in 1910. The design of the E6-class locomotive included

OPPOSITE and LEFT
Surviving locomotives are to be found in all sizes and conditions, the latter differing from the slightly dilapidated aspect presented by No. 5629, which has been left in the open, and the beautifully maintained No. 611, displayed at the U.S.A. 2000 exhibition.

another refinement, in the form of superheating. This was a development by a German engineer, Wilhelm Schmidt, and involved collecting the steam in the normal way but then ducting it through elements inside the firetubes so that it was superheated to much greater temperatures and pressures before being admitted to the cylinders. With the addition of superheating in 1910, the E6 locomotive developed 2,400hp (1789kW), which for its weight of 110 tons made it one of the most powerful locomotives ever built. The E6-class locomotives remained in use until after the end of World War II.

The Atlantic-type locomotives of the Pennsylvania Railroad did not employ the Wootten firebox but rather the square-topped Belpaire type for the better burning of the bituminous coal to which the Pennsylvania Railroad had easier access than did the Philadelphia & Reading Railroad. The latter therefore retained the Wootten firebox, and in the course of 1915 added a four-wheel trailing truck to produce a 4-4-4 type. Apart from some high-speed machines built for special services with lightweight trains during the 1930s, this was the last development of the four-coupled passenger engine, but the four-wheel trailing truck, in fact, fulfilled its true potential only in other applications.

For mainline passenger operations, the next type of major significance in the development of American railroad operations was the Pacific type of 4-6-2 locomotive. A slightly earlier type, the

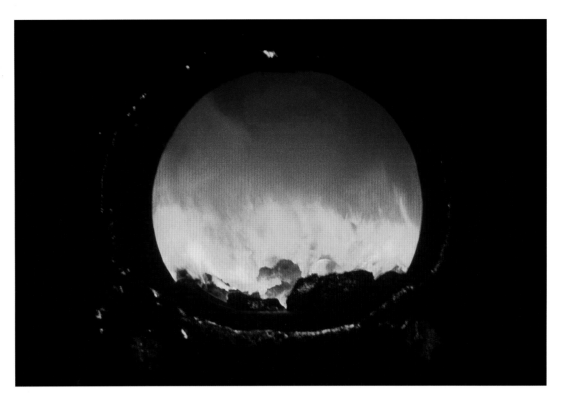

The heart of any steam locomotive is the combination of the firebox and boiler. The heat generated by the burning coal, much boosted by a carefully conceived draft mechanism, is ducted through pipes in the boiler to raise the temperature of the water contained in the boiler, until it reaches or passes the boiling point of water. The pressure of the steam is then employed to drive the pistons that turn the driving wheels.

Prairie type of 2-6-2 configuration had, like the 2-4-2 type that paved the way for the Atlantic type, revealed itself to be unstable at higher speeds. It is worth noting, though, that examples of the Prairie type of locomotive built in the first decade of the 20th century had been some of the largest passenger locomotives in the world at this time. The first Pacific-type locomotives were built for the Missouri Pacific Railroad in 1902, this design origin and primary region of operation providing the derivation of their generic name. Again, it was the Pennsylvania Railroad which produced the most impressive examples of this type, and again the new wheel configuration was combined with

other innovations to create a peak of development.

The Pennsylvania Railroad's first Pacific-type locomotives were the units of the K2-class that first appeared in 1907. These were based on a conventional arrangement of cylinders outside the wheels of the leading truck, controlled by a Stephenson-type link motion located between the wheels. This was then replaced by another type of link motion, named after its Belgian inventor, Egide Walschaert, operating outside the wheels and using sturdier rugged piston valves. By 1914 the original K2-class had been developed into the K4-class by the addition of the Walschaert gear. Although

Steam locomotives came in all sizes and shapes suited to a host of different tasks. At the lower end of the size scale were small saddle-tank units, such as that seen on the left, while at the upper end were the altogether larger, heavier and more powerful units used for hauling passenger and freight trains.

only 15 per cent heavier than its predecessor, the K4-class locomotive developed 33 per cent more tractive effort, and proved particularly effective on the Pennsylvania Railroad's line linking New York and Chicago, typified by some heavy grades. The addition of a mechanical stoking system during the 1920s allowed the K4-class locomotives to operate at maximum capability, which had proved impossible except on short runs when the delivery of coal to the firebox had been the

task of a man; as the weight of trains being hauled rose, the locomotives of the class were provided with tenders carrying 24,400 U.S. gal (92720 litres) of water as well as 25 tons of fuel.

On the route between New York and Chicago, the Pennsylvania Railroad's main opposition was the New York Central Railroad. This operated a longer but somewhat easier route that ran beside the Hudson river and Erie Canal to the shores of the Great Lakes, whereas the

The sight, sound and smell of a steam locomotive at full speed produced in the watcher a blend of sensations impossible to find elsewhere.

Pennsylvania Railroad operated on the direct route across the mountains. The New York Central Railroad also developed a series of Pacific-type locomotives, beginning with its first models in 1905, to take advantage of the operator's easier route through the running of heavier trains. A series of New York Central Railroad Pacific-type locomotives culminated in the K5-class that appeared in 1925, and an indication of the work required from them is given by the carriage of 15,000 U.S. gal (57000 litres) of water in their tenders.

The locomotives of the K5-class were very close to the limits of what could be achieved with the concept inherent in the Pacific-type. Thus the need for a still more capable and therefore heavier locomotive resulted during 1927 in the introduction of the first locomotive of 4-6-4 configuration, known as the Hudson-type after the location of the New York Central Railroad's main line out of New York. The four-wheel trailing truck permitted the use of a larger grate, and the Baker valve gear, a development of the Walschaert-type, was introduced on later models. Another feature of the Hudson type of locomotive, and one that had earlier appeared on the Pacific-type locomotives of the New York Central Railroad, was a small booster engine on the trailing truck to provide additional power for starting.

The original J1 class of Hudson-type locomotives were steadily improved over time, and reached their apogee in the J3 class of streamlined locomotives. The units

of this class secured an enduring fame as the locomotives that hauled the classic *Twentieth Century Limited* services between New York and Chicago during the later part of the 1930s. But the New York Central Railroad needed locomotives of still greater power, and this requirement led to the creation of the Niagara type of 4-8-4 locomotives. The Niagara-type was a development of the Mohawk type of 4-8-2 freight engines via the L3-class 4-8-2 locomotives that had showed themselves able to reach speeds of more than 80mph (129km/h), even with the relatively small wheels that were standard for freight locomotives.

These were only a very small percentage of the locomotive types, great and small, effective and not so effective,

that saw service with the U.S.A.'s still-considerable number of independent railroads. To take just one example, on the Milwaukee Road there had been a similar strain of development. First there had been a series of 4-6-0 locomotives during the 1890s, and both these and the following Atlantic-type locomotives that followed them used the Vauclain system of power-compounding. In 1907, however, there appeared the first of another type of Atlantic locomotive with the balanced system of compounding. This 1907 pattern of locomotive had two high-pressure and two low-pressure cylinders, but rather than locating them in pairs one above the other outside the leading truck wheels, the balanced system mounted the pair of low-pressure cylinders inside the frames. From

this position, they drove the axle of the leading pair of driving wheels, cranked for the purpose, while the high-pressure cylinders drove the leading coupled wheels in the conventional fashion. This type of balanced compounding was more complicated than 'simple' compounding and was also more difficult to maintain, so it never gained more than transitory popularity with American railroad operators. The fact that balanced compounding was by no means perfect or cost-effective is reflected in the fact that the Milwaukee Road reverted to the Vauclain pattern of compounding on its last class of Atlantic-type locomotives, which appeared in 1908. In 1910 the Milwaukee Road introduced its first Pacific-type locomotives in the form of the units of the F3-class, and these were followed by the locomotives of the F4-class during the next two years and then by the units of the F5-class with superheating. Production of the three F-class locomotives totalled 160 units, and the earlier engines were gradually upgraded to the definitive standard with superheating.

After it had opened its route to Tacoma and Seattle on the western seaboard of the U.S.A., the Milwaukee Road was faced with the problems of satisfying the differing demands of its transcontinental route, of which some parts were electrified and most parts were prone to the most adverse weather conditions; also of its shorter but considerably more competitive routes such

OPPOSITE
*This well streamlined
locomotive was operated by
the Norfolk & Western
Railroad.*

LEFT
*The red and orange livery of
the Southern Pacific
Railroad is strikingly
apparent in this photograph
of a passenger service hauled
by locomotive No. 4449.*

Now preserved as a museum exhibit, the streamliner locomotive No. 490 was built in 1926 and was a 4-6-2 unit of the F19 class, but was rebuilt in 1946 as a 4-6-4 unit of the L1 class to haul the Chessie *service of the Chesapeake & Ohio Railroad. The locomotive now stands at the Baltimore & Ohio Museum in Baltimore, Maryland.*

as those to Milwaukee, St. Paul and Omaha. Until the later part of the 1920s the Milwaukee Road employed Pacific-type locomotives on both types of its services, but then in 1929 there appeared a new class of locomotive with 4-6-4 wheel configuration. The new locomotives soon proved themselves to be very fast: in July 1934 such a locomotive employed on a special high-speed run on the 86-mile (138-km) line between Chicago and Milwaukee recorded an average of 92.3mph (148.5km/h) on a segment of 65.6 miles (105.6km), and a maximum speed of 103.5mph (166.6km/h).

For the long runs typical of the route to the Pacific coast, a more powerful type, the S1 class of 4-8-4 locomotives was introduced. The first of these was delivered by Baldwin in 1930 and, with a tractive force of more than 62,000lb (28123kg) by comparison with the 45,820lb (20874kg) of the F6 class of 4-6-4-type locomotives, was more than capable of hauling the heaviest of passenger trains. In the 1930s the Milwaukee Road introduced its celebrated streamlined *Hiawatha* services, and for the route between Chicago and Minneapolis with six cars, the American Locomotive Company (Alco) in 1935 produced the A class of 4-4-2 locomotives. The A-class locomotive was able to maintain a speed higher than 100mph (161km/h), and its success meant that the Milwaukee Road soon increased the *Hiawatha* service first to nine and finally to 12 cars, even though this meant a modest degradation in overall

performance. This led to the introduction in 1938 of the F7 class of 4-6-4 locomotives which were able to haul even a 12-car train at a maximum speed of more than 120mph (193km/h), and was employed for one of the fastest steam-hauled scheduled services in the world, the section of the route linking Minneapolis and Milwaukee between Sparta and Portage, which was covered at an average speed of 81mph (130.4km/h).

Another outstanding class of locomotives of the late 1930s was the Atchison, Topeka & Santa Fe Railroad's 3771 class of 4-8-4 engines, which were used on the 1,790-mile (2880-km) route linking Kansas City and Los Angeles.

These locomotives were able to undertake the one-way trip in 26 hours, and could be readied for the return trip in only a few hours.

By this stage of the development of American railroads, where a technical peak had been achieved in the development of steam locomotives but the operating railroads were coming under other increasing financial pressures through the emergence of other forms of long-distance and high-speed travel, the aspect of locomotive operation that was now in the highest demand was not so much outright performance as the combination of high performance with the minimum possible servicing and

RIGHT
The Denver & Rio Grande
Zephyr *rolls into Glenwood*
Springs, Colorado on its
westbound run to Salt Lake
City in Utah in 1980.

OPPOSITE
This diesel-hauled service of
the Burlington Northern
Railroad includes one single-
and five double-deck
passenger cars, a reflection of
the railroad's need to move
large numbers of short-range
commuter passengers
without recourse to trains
too long for existing
platforms.

maintenance requirements. It is worth noting that the steam locomotive's ability to deliver power and speed had reached the point at which further developments along these dimensions of performance could not be considered as a result of the limitations imposed by the nature of the track.

Another threat to the steam-powered locomotive at this time was posed by the diesel-engined locomotive. This was a comparatively new type, but already it was beginning to rival the steam-powered locomotive in terms of performance and, perhaps more importantly, in terms of instant availability for service when required, without the need for a period in which to light the fire and heat the water to operating temperature.

One of the ultimate expressions of American steam-locomotive development that appeared at this time, was the New York Central Railroad's Niagara type of engine, which was designed with the very high 6,000hp (4474kW) and also a power/weight ratio better than that offered by the railroad's current 4-6-4 locomotives. This object was achieved by the combination of a number of factors, including the omission of a steam dome to allow the introduction of a boiler of greater diameter, the enlargement of the firebox, steam passages and superheater elements, the use of higher-strength carbon steel where appropriate, and the introduction of roller bearings. To allow full exploitation of the design's capabilities, driving wheels with

OPPOSITE
A General Electric Class 44T Bo-Bo No.16, built in May 1945, shunts SW7 Bo-Bo No. 331 off the turntable at the Bangor depot, Maine, and into the roundhouse stall.

LEFT
Chicago & North Western Railroad push/pull double-deck commutor train leaves Chicago for Vermont Street.

diameters of 75 and 79in (1.905 and 2.0m) were supplied. Appearing in 1945, the S1 class of Niagara-type locomotives was used on the route linking New York and Chicago, regularly working the 930-mile (1497-km) distance from Harmon, where they took over from the electric locomotives that brought the trains out of Grand Central Station, to Chicago. The railroad undertook a very rigorous comparative examination of the performance and operating economics of the S1-class steam locomotives and comparable diesel locomotives: the six S1-class locomotives had availability and utilization rates of 76 and 69 per cent respectively, amounting to the ability to cover 260,000 miles (418420km) per year, while the diesel locomotives, which were nearly twice as expensive to purchase, offered the typicality to cover 330,000 miles (531070km).

Thus there was a limited case for the continued use of the S1-class locomotives, but there were problems with the high-strength/low-weight steel that had been used for the manufacture of their boilers, which soon began to crack. The New York Central Railroad then decided that the reboilering programme that would be required would not offer a good return on the requirement investment, and abandoned its last steam-powered locomotives in favour of diesel-engined locomotives for its next generation of engine. Within only a few years more,

RIGHT
The Denver & Rio Grande
Zephyr *comes out of the*
west portal of the Moffat
Tunnel at Winter Park in
Colorado on its run from
Denver to Salt Lake City in
Utah.

virtually every American railroad had followed the same course and the steam-powered locomotive retreated into history.

In parallel with steam-powered locomotives for the hauling of passenger services, there took place the steady evolution of the same type of locomotive for freight-hauling purposes. As early as 1842 Matthias Baldwin had created the design of an 0-8-0 dedicated freight locomotive for the Georgia Central Railroad. This was too complex in its mechanical details for its adoption by more than a very limited number of operators, but it nonetheless showed that the use of larger numbers of smaller wheels was the way in which an effective freight-hauling locomotive should be designed.

A railroad whose operations were in considerable need of increased power was the Central Pacific Railroad, whose line included a steep climb from Sacramento into the Sierra Nevada mountains; in 1882 A.J. Stevens created an effective 4-8-0 design, of which 20 were manufactured for the Central Pacific Railroad. In 1883 Stevens expanded on this original concept to produce the 4-10-0 locomotive named *El Gobernador*, but this huge engine turned the scales at 65 tons and was thus too heavy for the track of the period and remained a prototype, albeit the largest locomotive in the world, rather than a working engine.

In the last part of the 19th century, Mogul- and Consolidation-type locomotives, of 2-6-0 and 2-8-0 layouts

A New York Central diesel-hauled passenger service proceeds on its way to or from one of the system's metropolitan destinations.

respectively, became the standard types for freight operations. The latter was generally more successful and popular, and among the most powerful of such locomotives at the beginning of the 20th century were two that were manufactured in 1900 by the Pittsburgh Locomotive Works for the Bessemer & Lake Erie Railroad's iron ore-carrying operation. Weighing more than 110 tons and

developing a tractive effort of almost 64,000lb (29030kg), these locomotives were created to work the heavily graded line between the railroad's docks at Conneaut and its yard at Albion. Others of the same manufacturer's 2-8-0 locomotives, for use on less steeply graded sections of the same operator's line, were less massive at a weight of 79 tons, or slightly more, with tractive effort of 38,400lb (17420kg).

The principle advantage offered by the eight-coupled layout was the concentration of the weight on the driving-wheels, which provided greater adhesion and thus improved tractive effort. An indication of the popularity of the type in the early part of the 20th century was the series of orders, totalling 680 units, placed by the government of the U.S.A. for locomotives of the type for

The New York Central Railroad 4-8-2 freight train No. 3113, passing through Dunkirk, New York in 1952.

military service in France during World War I. Such was the manufacturing effort devoted to this high-priority programme that by a time early in 1918 no fewer than 30 locomotives were being completed every day. By this time, still larger locomotives were being adopted for regular use.

There was not the same speed requirement for freight locomotives as there was for passenger locomotives, so two-wheel leading trucks were standard, even though some operators did prefer four-wheel trucks: the Pennsylvania Railroad, as just a single example, during 1918 introduced the first of an extensive

series of 4-8-2 locomotives for fast freight duties. The series reached its peak in 1930 with the M1a-class, whose units each weighed 342 tons, including the tender, and offered a tractive effort of 64,550lb (29280kg).

More commonly used was the freight locomotive counterpart of the Pacific-type passenger engine. This was the Mikado type of 2-8-2 configuration, and was the single type of freight locomotive manufactured in the largest numbers: production totalled some 9,500 units compared with manufacture of about 22,000 2-8-0 locomotives. The Atchison, Topeka & Santa Fe Railroad took the

process one step further in 1903 with the introduction of its 2-10-2 locomotive, which used the trailing truck to give greater flexibility on the railroad's sections over mountainous terrain, characterized by steep grades and tight curves.

From the use of a trailing truck with two wheels it was natural to evolve toward a truck with four wheels, so that a firebox of greater size could be supported. During the mid-1920s, eight- and 10-coupled locomotives of this layout were created. The 2-10-4 configuration was known to American operators as the Texas-type, as the first such engine was built to the order of the Texas & Pacific

A Pennsylvania Railroad 2-10-0 descending Horseshoe Curve at Altoona, after banking.

Railroad in 1925, and to Canadian operators as the Selkirk-type, as they were first used in this mountain region of western Canada from 1929. The 2-8-4 freight locomotive was first used by the New York Central Railroad in 1925, and this led to the general use of the designation Berkshire type after the mountain range of that name in the western part of Massachusetts.

Certainly numbered among the largest non-articulated freight locomotives must be the 4-10-2 and 4-12-2 engines manufactured by Alco for the Union Pacific Railroad and delivered for service from 1926. The four-wheel pilot trucks

allowed the use of three cylinders, which maximized the power that could be obtained without resorting to articulation. Weighing 350 tons, the 90 examples of the 4-12-2 type each delivered a tractive effort of 96,600lb (43820kg) and could work 3,800-ton trains at an average speed of 35mph (56.5km/h).

Largest of all steam locomotives, however, were the articulated units. The particular articulation system employed for locomotives used on American railroads was that developed in France by Anatole Mallet in the later part of the 19th century. This was based on a single boiler supplying steam to two sets of cylinders.

This steam was used first by two high-pressure cylinders and then delivered to two low-pressure cylinders. The main feature differentiating the Mallet system from other compound systems, however, was the employment of two sets of driving wheels on separate chassis: the leading chassis was arranged so that it could turn and swivel, thus improving the ability of the whole locomotive to negotiate curves without problem.

The first Mallet type of locomotive manufactured in North America was built by Alco and delivered to the Baltimore & Ohio Railroad in 1904. Within just a few years of this, the Mallet type of locomotive

had became very popular with operators running heavy freight services. As the number of driving wheels on Mallet-type locomotives was increased from 12 to 16 and even 20, leading and trailing trucks were added to enhance riding qualities and later, to provide adequate support, a larger firebox. The most popular layout for Mallet-type locomotives in North America was 2-6-6-2, but the largest of all of these were the 4-8-8-4 Big Boy units delivered to the Union Pacific Railroad from 1941. At 354 tons, these were the heaviest steam locomotives ever made. They were not the most powerful of all locomotives, but the Big Boys were fast and operationally efficient and, like the preceding Challenger-type 4-6-6-4 units, could haul express freight trains at up to 50mph (80.5km/h). The Big Boy locomotives were unexcelled on the Union Pacific Railroad's route through the mountains between Ogden and Cheyenne, a section on which they ensured timely delivery of fruit trains between Ogden and Green river, where Challenger-type locomotives took over. Like the later Mallet types operated by other American railroads, both of these Union Pacific Railroad types dispensed with compounding after the low-pressure cylinders had become so large that they could no longer be installed, and the valves had become inadequate to deal with the volume of steam.

There were many variants on the theme of the Mallet-type locomotive. In 1914, for example, the Erie Railroad received the first of three 2-8-8-8-2 Triplex

OPPOSITE
This diesel-hauled service operated in the Napa Valley region of California under the banner Napa Valley Wine Train, *in acknowledgement of the region's primary industry.*

LEFT
Preserved in the museum at Sacramento, California, locomotive No. 347C was a unit of the Santa Fe Western Railroad's fleet.

Mallet locomotives, of a pattern developed by Baldwin and carrying a second set of low-pressure cylinders on the tender, for service as a helper. The addition of extra cylinders without extra steam-generating capacity was a factor that militated against the general success of the Triplex concept. A 2-8-8-8-4 unit with a larger boiler and slightly smaller cylinders was delivered to the Virginian Railroad, but suffered from the same type of limitation as the Triplex. The same lack of overall success attended

the 2-10-10-2 units of the Atchison, Topeka & Santa Fe Railroad: these were rebuilt to this configuration from earlier locomotives, and were characterized by jointed boilers. More successful, though, were the 10 examples of a 2-10-10-2 type that the Virginian Railroad bought, despite its unhappy experience with the Triplex, to help 6,000-ton coal-carrying trains up an 11-mile (17.7-km) stretch of 2 per cent grades in the Allegheny mountains. Two other operators which had considerable

success with Mallet-type locomotives in mountainous terrain were the Denver & Rio Grande Western Railroad, which operated locomotives of this articulated type on its difficult main lines in the Rockies, and the Southern Pacific Railroad that developed a cab-first locomotive for service in the Sierra Nevada mountain section of its line linking California and Nevada. Their use of oil rather than coil fuel made it possible for 4-8-8-2 locomotives of this type, of which 195

were completed between 1928 and 1944, to run backwards in an unusual arrangement with the tender trailing and the engineer thereby enjoying an unhindered forward field of vision.

The Mallet type of locomotive was the largest type of steam locomotive ever built in North America, and it was also among the last of the breed to be manufactured. In the period following the end of World War II, American railroad operators turned quite swiftly to the use of diesel-engined locomotives, but the Norfolk & Western Railroad, involved primarily in the movement of coal from the mining area of Kentucky and West Virginia, tried to improve its locomotives to offer operational availability and efficiency

RIGHT

*This is a caboose unit of the
Burlington Northern
Railroad, the raised section
having being designed to
provide the conductor with
good fields of vision.*

BELOW RIGHT

*Caboose 662 of Maine
Central Railroad at Bangor,
Maine*

OPPOSITE

*SW11 Bo-Bo Switcher No.
55 of the Seattle & North
Coast Railroad stands on the
quayside of the East
Waterway in Seattle,
Washington.*

equal to that of diesel-engined
locomotives. In its own facilities, the
Norfolk & Western designed and built
three new models. The J class of 4-8-4
locomotives was delivered from 1941 as a
type optimized for the working of prestige
passenger services at 100mph (161km/h)
or more, while the A and Y classes of
2-6-6-4 and 2-8-8-2 articulated
locomotives, dating from 1936 and 1948
respectively, were an optimized freight-
hauling service, the A-class unit at speeds
up to 70mph (112.5km/h) and the Y6-class
unit for heavier loads at lower speeds. The
real advance with these and the Y6b-type,
the final development of the Mallet
concept, was the complete rationalization
of maintenance so that less than an hour
was needed for a total inspection,
refuelling and lubrication between runs:
the maintenance cost of the Y6b-class
locomotive was a significant 37 per cent
lower than that of the preceding Y5-class
locomotives.

Even so, the Norfolk & Western
Railroad could not stem the apparently
inexorable progress of the diesel-engined
locomotive. The Y6b-class locomotive was
manufactured up to 1952, but the Norfolk
& Western had itself contracted for the
delivery of 75 diesel-engined locomotives
by 1957. The operator's last steam
locomotive, and the last such engine
completed for any mainline American
railroad, was an 0-8-0 switcher completed
in 1953. Then the problems of maintaining
a fleet of steam-engined locomotives,
when the rest of the national industry had

turned over to diesel power, finally caught up with the Norfolk & Western, and in 1960 steam operations were ended with a final run by a Y6b locomotive on 4 April of that year.

This is only one, albeit the core aspect, of steam locomotion in the U.S.A., for there were many types of steam locomotive other than those that worked main-line passenger and freight services. Some of these other types were efforts to extend the life of steam as a practical form of motive power, and a typical example is the use of steam turbines, with which a small number of railroads experimented in and around the time of World War II. One such aspect of turbine development was the 6-8-6 geared turbine locomotive that the Pennsylvania Railroad tested in 1944: this saw a limited amount of operational service but had no long-term effect on the decline of steam power. Another way in which steam was applied to railroad operations was in the form of the generation of electricity powering motors on the driving axles. Experiments along this line were undertaken in 1938 by the Union Pacific Railroad, in 1947 by the Chesapeake & Ohio Railroad, and in 1952 by the Norfolk & Western.

An earlier type of locomotive, based on the use of geared transmission, was created for the specific task of operations on the extemporized railroads associated with the logging industry. Named for the engineer who created the first such engine in 1880, the Shay type of locomotive remained in production until 1945; its

LOCOMOTIVES & ROLLING STOCK

ABOVE
A three-car turbo train on a demonstration run at Springfield, Massachusetts.

OPPOSITE
The Napa Valley Railroad operated its services in a livery somewhat more discreet than those worn by many other American railroads.

manufacture was the foundation stone of the Lima Locomotive Works, which then became one of the major manufacturers of steam locomotives in the U.S.A., with Baldwin and Alco its two main rivals.

The chain-driven Robb was another type of steam locomotive, this time with a tilted boiler, but again optimized for use by the logging industry, and was developed in Canada for construction from 1903 to run on timber tracks. Two other unusual types were the Heeler and the Climax, also for use in the logging industry: the former had a V- cylinder arrangement and was driven by a central shaft and universal couplings, and the latter had a combination of chains and gears.

These were all very specialized locomotives, but within the standard railroad operations there were large numbers of smaller steam locomotives to undertake little-sung but nonetheless vital support tasks. Such, for example, were the vast numbers of 0-6-0 and 0-8-0 switching engines that were employed to make up trains in the classification yards: these were often obsolete engines past their prime and relegated from the main lines to the yards; but many were purpose-built for the bigger railroads.

Electric power possesses a number of features that make it very attractive for the purposes of railroad service. Despite this fact, there was never any chance that

310

OPPOSITE
A northbound Chessie System coal train of 148 hoppers and caboose in West Virginia.

LEFT
A diesel-hauled service of the Southern Pacific Railroad passes through Jack London Square in Oakland, California, in this photograph of April 1999.

OPPOSITE
*A colourful picture as B30-7
No. 8273, GP40 No. 4176
and GP40-2 No. 4409 haul a
northbound Chessie System
train of 190 empty coal
hoppers in the New river
valley, West Virginia.*

LEFT
*A triple-headed diesel service
of the Southern Pacific
Railroad moves sedately
along the Shasta, California
route.*

electric power could replace steam power on a one-for-one basis on the American railroad system. The primary reason for this is that electricity is useful only if it can be delivered to the engine fitted with the relevant electric motors, and there was never a realistic possibility of this happening in the North American continent. Even as much of the railway system in Europe was being electrified in the 20th century, America was still expanding to its maximum extent of some 250,000 miles (402325km), and even the thought of electrifying this type of mileage was impossible to contemplate.

Even so, the quiet operation and lack of pollution associated with electric power made the concept of electric trains attractive for a number of applications.

The ability of the electric motor to operate for short times at well over its nominal rating also opened the way to train operations in locations where cost or other difficulties might otherwise have made such operation impossible. The third area in which electric locomotion has found a major application is in regions in which the traffic volume is high enough or the electricity cost low enough to make the reduction in operating costs greater than the initially high equipment expenses.

Experiments in the use of electricity for the movement of vehicles were comparatively common in the 19th century, and in 1880 an experimental electric tram service was trialled in Toronto. But the first main-line electrification was undertaken only in 1895

LOCOMOTIVES & ROLLING STOCK

RIGHT and OPPOSITE
These types of multiple-head services are typical of the very heavy freighting operations that are common in modern American railroad operations for the movement of bulk freight loads.

in Baltimore after the city fathers had ordered the Baltimore & Ohio to cease their use of steam locomotives within the city limits. The railroad therefore modified a 7-mile (11.25-km) length of track, including the tunnel beneath the Patapsco river, with a 650-volt DC overhead electric supply system so that 1,080-hp (805-kW) locomotives could haul trains into and out of the centre of the city.

The aim of Baltimore in forcing this change on the Baltimore & Ohio Railroad was to reduce noise and pollution in the city's heavily populated centre. The same reason was behind the thinking of the authorities in New York city when they too demanded that steam locomotion be removed from the central part of the city: steam locomotives were banned from Manhattan Island from 1908, and by that

time the New York Central Railroad had electrified its approaches to Grand Central Station over the 20 miles (32km) from Harmon, while the New York, New Haven & Hartford line had been converted by 1907, initially to Stamford in Connecticut and then to New Haven in the same state. However, it was the Pennsylvania Railroad that undertook the most ambitious electrification scheme in the

316

RIGHT
This unit was operated by Sperry Rail Services for development purposes.

OPPOSITE
Galloping Goose *No. 3, previously of the Rio Grande Southern Railroad, now situated at Knotts Berry Farm, Los Angeles.*

Snowploughs belonging to the Maine Central Railroad at its Bangor Yard.

New York area after this operator's purchase of Long Island Rail Road in 1900: the Long Island line itself was electrified in 1905, and the Pennsylvania Railroad's system of tunnels, which allowed it to create its new terminus at Pennsylvania Station, included a through connection with the Long Island system. The Pennsylvania Railroad extended

electrification to the suburban commuter lines of Philadelphia from 1915, and by 1933 was operating electric trains between Philadelphia and New York, with Washington, D.C. added by 1935, when this electrified system comprised 364 route miles (586 route km) with 1,405 miles (2261km) of track.

Tunnels were another feature of

railroad systems that were immediately attractive as objects for electrification, as this would remove the need for heavy maintenance to mitigate the corrosive effects of discharged smoke and also the need to provide ventilation to remove the smoke. Thus the St. Clair River Tunnel between Port Huron and Sarnia on the Grand Trunk Railway of Canada's cross-

Conrail's Hurricane jet snow blower No. 740 at Newark, New Jersey. It was built by the Railway Maintenance Corporation of Pittsburg.

border operation into Michigan came to have electric traction in 1908, and in 1909 the Great Northern's Cascade Tunnel and its approaches were electrified. The Boston & Maine Railroad's Hoosick Tunnel was electrified in 1911, and the Mount Royal Tunnel to the Canadian National Railway Company's station in the centre of Montreal was operated by electric

locomotives as soon as it had been completed a few years later. Further electrification arrived in the 1920s, such as in the 7.8-mile (12.6-km) Cascade Tunnel that was part of a system that embraced a total of 72 miles (116km) of track, in the Michigan Central Railroad's tunnel at Detroit, and on the Illinois Central Railroad's suburban lines in Chicago.

The use of electric locomotives also came to be more prominent on sections of routes where steam locomotion presented unacceptable difficulties or operating expense. The classic example of this was the 656 miles (1056km) of main line operated by the Milwaukee Road in the Rocky and Bitter Root Mountains, and the Norfolk & Western and the Virginian

RIGHT and OPPOSITE
*Continued operational
capability in the winter
months over large parts of
the U.S.A. depends on the
use of special plough
locomotives to keep the
tracks clear of snow. These
have to be sited in the areas
most likely to be affected by
heavy snowfalls, and must be
kept ready to move out at a
moment's notice. Both of the
equipments illustrated here
are of the rotary type,
designed to draw the snow
into the maw of the rotor and
then eject it to the side.*

Railroads also converted to electric traction to overcome problems with operating conditions. The Norfolk & Western Railroad electrified a 30-mile (48-km) section of its line linking Bluefield and Vivian, where steam locomotives were finding it very difficult to work 4,000-ton coal trains over 2 per cent grades, and also through the Elkhorn Tunnel: the initial scheme of 1915 was very successful, and in 1926 was extended to Williamson. The line was later rebuilt with reduced grades and a new tunnel, and electric working was then abandoned. The Virginian Railroad had similar problems on its line linking Mullins and Roanoke, so in the 1920s it supplanted the Mallet-type locomotives currently used on this section with powerful electric locomotives that could handle coal trains of up to 16,000 tons.

What is abundantly evident in the early phases of American railroad electrification is that it suffered from the

RIGHT

A newcomer to electric train operations in 1906 was this Baldwin-Westinghouse-built locomotive, designed to operate on both direct and alternating currents (direct current over the New York Central line and alternating current on the New Haven). This type of locomotive is capable of handling a 200-ton train in local service at an average speed of 26mph (42km/h). The maximum needed to maintain this average speed was about 45mph (72km/h).

RIGHT

This electrically-powered unit with diagonally-angled brushes was an early attempt to provide for the automatic clearance of lines of snow and falling leaves.

OPPOSITE

This Wolfeborough Railroad unit was an early attempt to create a rapid transit capability for local services in New Hampshire.

same factors that had bedevilled the first stages of railroad construction in general: everything was undertaken on the basis of individual operators without any thought for the integration of piecemeal developments, with detrimental effects on any efforts at research and development. These initial drawbacks were compounded by the greater durability of electric railway systems, which meant that there was little incentive to create any rationalized systems. These problems inevitably came home to roost, as is indicated by the experience of Amtrak when it schemed the renewal of the electrified route between Washington and New York and the extension of this route to Boston: the Pennsylvania Railroad uses a 12,000-volt 25-cycle AC system on the route linking Washington and New York, the line to New Haven has been renewed and extended to Boston using 25,000-volt electricity, but in New York the Metropolitan Transportation Authority uses 12,500-volt 60-cycle current! If an integrated service linking Washington with Boston via New York is to be created, Amtrak must replace at least part of the electricity supply to the route, or alternatively purchase locomotives able to use any of the three different types of electrical current.

Expense has long been the limiting factor in attempts to increase the length of electrified railroad. Another operator who has baulked at the cost is CP Rail, which wanted to electrify its lines in the mountain regions in the west of Canada.

RIGHT and BELOW
Amtrak's Desert Wind
stands at Union Station in
Ogden, Utah.

The greater power and traction provided by electricity would have gone a long way to solving CP Rail's problems in the mountains, as well as reducing fuel costs, but it was decided that the expense was prohibitive.

Even so, some industrial lines have been built in recent times with electric traction to allow automation. The Carol Lake iron ore mines in the north-eastern part of Quebec use a 6-mile (9.7-km) track to ferry ore to the crushing plant, and other examples are the 15-mile (24-km) Muskingham Electric Railroad in Ohio and the 78-mile (125.5-km) Black Mesa &

Lake Powell Railroad, the latter using 6,000-hp (4474-kW) locomotives to haul 8,000-ton coal trains.

In the event, the requirements that were first satisfied by some aspects of electrification were removed by the appearance of diesel-engined traction. The Milwaukee Road's electric sections became an inconvenience after the diesel-engined locomotive had proved its ability to operate successfully over the whole of the operator's route network in the north-western part of the U.S.A., and several other electric operations, including that of the Norfolk & Western Railroad, were terminated after the grades that had led to their initial implementation had been rebuilt to easier standards. The new type of locomotion, which wholly supplanted steam locomotion and also caused the abandonment of many aspects of electric locomotion, removed the primary objection to large-scale electrification, namely the huge cost of installing the power-supply system, through the combination of the flexibility provided by electric traction and the installation of the electricity-generating equipment on board the locomotive.

The diesel engine was patented by its German inventor in 1892, but it was 20 more years before a successful method was found to overcome the main handicap of the diesel engine for use in railroad applications, namely the method in which the power of the engine could be utilized. A number of transmission systems were developed and evaluated, but the most

LEFT
The second man in the cab of locomotive No. 224 is about to collect train orders from the post at Mission Tower Junction, as the San Diegan *heads south on Santa Fe tracks after pushing back out of Union Station in Los Angeles.*

Great Northern Railway's streamliner, Empire Builder *No. 5018, travelling alongside the Wenatchee river near Wenatchee, Washington, in electrified territory. The locomotive develops 5,000hp. This and an identical one which Great Northern also has are the largest single-cab all-electric locomotives in the world.*

Great Northern's 5,000-hp locomotive is pulling a freight train which is leaving the eastern portal of the 7.79-mile (12.5-km) Cascade Tunnel near Berne, Washington.

commonly accepted of these, and the one accepted to the exclusion of all others for service on American railroads, is the employment of the diesel engine for the generation of electricity, which is then used to power axle-mounted electric motors. In the U.S.A. it was in 1924 that the General Electric company produced a 300-hp (224-kW) Bo-Bo, which is two pairs of axles, each with its own motor, and this engine and its derivatives were later adopted by many railroads for use in switching tasks. These early machines had a poor power/weight ratio, the original 300-hp (224-kW) switcher weighing some 60 tons. A similar power/weight ratio on a locomotive for main-line service would have made it too heavy for practical use. The early diesel-engined locomotives were

also considerably more costly to buy than the equivalent steam locomotives, though this factor was counterbalanced by their use of considerably cheaper fuel.

There were many experimental developments during the 1920s and 1930s, and one that was pioneered at this time came to yield very significant dividends. This line of approach was started by the Electromotive and Winston Engine companies, which became a division of General Motors in 1930 and concentrated its efforts on the development and manufacture of a lightweight diesel-engined powerplant, the 201A: possessing a much improved power/weight ratio, the 201A was first used in the celebrated *Zephyr* streamlined passenger train built for the Burlington Northern Railroad in

LEFT and BELOW
Two further views of Great Northern's Empire Builder, one of two owned by the company. The two identical locomotives were designed primarily for heavy mountain duty. Each is 101-ft long (31m) and weighs 360 tons.

that could compete on level terms with current steam locomotives.

The first sales of the new type of locomotive were made to the Baltimore & Ohio and the Atchison, Topeka & Santa Fe Railroads, and Electromotive then developed the 1800-hp (1342-kW) E1-class locomotive into the 2000-hp (1491-kW) E6-class type, which appeared in 1938. This basic design became the standard, and was manufactured in both cab and booster versions: the normal operational concept involved the use of two cab units with a booster between them to create a 6,000-hp (4474-kW) locomotive that could be driven from either end.

The versatility of the new units, together with their reduced fuel costs, lower maintenance requirements, and

OPPOSITE
The Burlington Railroad, Chicago in 1952, and the Denver Zephyr *is departing.*

LEFT
Atchison, Topeka & Santa Fe Railroad's El Capitan *at La Junta.*

BELOW LEFT
Atchison, Topeka & Santa Fe's San Francisco Chief *at Gallup, in New Mexico.*

1934. In May of that year, the *Zephyr* achieved a major proof of the diesel engine's capabilities when its completed the 1,015-mile (1633-km) run between Denver and Chicago, without a halt, in just over 13 hours. The three-car *Zephyr*, however, was a special lightweight train powered by a single 600-hp (447.5-kW) unit, so a more important breakthrough, which was achieved in the following year, was the occasion on which two of the new engines were mounted in a prototype locomotive for main-line operation. The eight-cylinder engines used in the *Zephyr* became 12-cylinder units, each rated at 900hp (6571kW) to give the locomotive a total of 1,800hp (1342kW); the coupling of two such units finally created something

RIGHT
The Coast Starlight *to Oakland, Portland and Seattle, leaving Los Angeles with Amtrak locomotives 569 and 567, in their old colour scheme, and running past Misson Tower Junction.*

RIGHT
The Coast Starlight *to Oakland, Portland and Seattle, leaving Los Angeles with Amtrak locomotives 569 and 567, in their old colour scheme, and running past Misson Tower Junction.*

OPPOSITE
Seen at Chicago in 1952, this is an EMD F-class tractor unit used to haul the operator's Super Chief *service.*

resultant higher levels of availability, made the diesel-engined locomotive increasingly attractive to American railroads. Another attractive feature of the diesel locomotive lay in the fact that while the steam locomotive, almost invariably designed to meet the particular need of a particular railroad, was difficult to sell to another operator, the standardized diesel locomotive could be used anywhere and was thus better security for the type of loan that was often required because of the type's higher purchase cost.

Over the next 25 years, nearly 1,300 examples of the E-class locomotive were delivered to railroads throughout the country, and so successful and durable were they that many survived to serve with Amtrak in the 1970s.

The next stage in diesel development was the creation of a more powerful locomotive optimized for use on freight services. By adapting the 567 engine used in the E6-class locomotive, Electromotive came up with a highly effective 16-cylinder engine rated at 1,350hp (1007kW). The combination of four units, in the form of two cab and two booster units, were combined to create a 5,400-hp (4026-kW) locomotive. This was evaluated as a special demonstration model, and the trials revealed fuel costs halved from those of an equivalent steam locomotive; a bonus was the new unit's ability to be used as separate 2,700-hp (2013-kW) combinations. The new locomotive was a great success right from the start, and its production development as the FT and F

RIGHT
Northern Pacific's streamlined North Coast Limited *leaving King Street station in Seattle at the start of its transcontinental trip to Chicago.*

BELOW RIGHT
Chicago & North Western streamliner Twin Cities 400 *on the curve just outside North Western Station in Chicago in 1939.*

OPPOSITE
Chicago, Burlington & Quincy Railroad's California Zephyr *at Omaha.*

classes resulted in the manufacture of almost 7,000 units.

During World War II, Electromotive was largely insulated from competition by a directive of the War Production Board, which stipulated that manufacture of railroad diesel locomotives should be left to this component of General Motors, while other firms concentrated on smaller types. Among these latter was the Alco, which had started production of a 2,000-hp (1491-kW) locomotive during 1940. In collaboration with General Electric, Alco had earlier manufactured large numbers of diesel-engined switchers, and during World War II was limited to the production of diesel units rated at 1,000hp (746kW) or less. Alco was not altogether defeated by the War Production Board's strictures, however, for it created a general-purpose type which became known as the road-switcher, which was basically a switching engine with provision for extra fuel and heating equipment so that it could also be employed for main-line freight and passenger work.

By the end of World War II in 1945, there was general acceptance of the fact that the diesel locomotive offered a complete range of operational and other advantages over the steam locomotive. Indeed, by 1948 the demand for new diesel locomotives was considerably more than the manufacturers could satisfy. By this time, Alco was back in competition for main-line business with 1,500-hp (1118-kW) road-switchers and 2000-hp (1491-

334

The Santa Fe Super Chief passing through Apache Canyon shortly after leaving Lamy, New Mexico on the eastbound run to Chicago.

kW) passenger locomotives, and Baldwin and Fairbanks-Morse had also begun the manufacture of commercial diesel locomotives. Electromotive remained the market leader, however, and by the late 1960s all of its original competitors had abandoned the commercial chase.

General Electric ended its partnership with Alco in 1953 and began to produce its own road-switchers. By this time, the road-switcher had gained universal acceptance as the best possible means of exploiting the diesel engine's inherent versatility; another step forward was the replacement of the cab body for the hood body. In its basic form, the hood type of diesel locomotive has a casing which covers the machinery but does not extend over the full width of the locomotive, which provides the full-width cab with adequate fields of vision for driving in each direction. The flexibility of operational capability provided by this type of locomotive was reflected in Electromotive's use of the basic designation of GP (general purpose) for its road-switchers. More than 6,000 of the 1500-hp (1118-kW) GP7-class and 1,750-hp (1305-kW) GP9-class locomotives were sold during the 1950s, and more potent models that appeared later included the 2,000-hp (1491-kW) GP20 and GP38 classes, and the 3,000-hp (2237-kW) GP40-class, which were manufactured in both cab and hood versions.

Power in the order of 3,000hp (2237kW) is now seen as the maximum useful power for a single unit. Much

bigger models have indeed been built, such as the 5,000-hp (3728-kW) types delivered to the Union Pacific Railroad during the early 1960s; but the diesel engine's capability for linking into multiple units adaptable to virtually every level of power requirement makes the concentration of so much power in a single locomotive a matter of poor economy. Even so, the Union Pacific Railroad went one step further on the power ladder during 1969 with its 6,600-hp (4921-kW) DDA40X-class unit, which was two standard units in a common case. The railroad purchased 47 units of this type up to 1971.

More recent ranges of diesel locomotives accept 3,500hp (2610kW) as the greatest desirable rating. Both Electromotive and General Electric produce units in this range, notably the former's four-axle GP50-class unit for fast freight services and the six-axle SD50-class unit for heavier duties, and the latter's 3,000-hp (2237-kW) C30-class and 3,600-hp (2684-kW) C36-class units.

Meanwhile, production of passenger locomotives slumped in line with the decline of passenger demand. One of the problems that Amtrak had to tackle on its establishment was how best to replace the elderly diesel locomotives, as well as other rolling stock, that it has inherited from the railroad operators who took the opportunity to free themselves of their loss-making passenger operations. Among the locomotives that required replacement were 286 examples of the E and F diesel

classes, the Pennsylvania Railroad's fleet of 40 GG-1-class electric locomotives from the 1930s, and the more modern Budd Metroliners. The first replacement for the diesel locomotives was the new Electromotive 3,000-hp (2237-kW) SPD40F cab version of the standard SD40-class locomotive. All efforts to run these six-axle units at high speed on poor-quality track, over which Amtrak has no control, unfortunately led to several derailments, resulting in the imposition of speed restrictions. The only possible solution to this operational problem was an expensive rebuilding process to convert the existing locomotives into four-axle models, and more such units were ordered with the revised designation of class F40PH.

In the absence of adequate contemporary electric locomotive designs for service on the electrified main line between New York and Washington, D.C., Amtrak resorted to the expedient of an adaptation of the General Electric freight engine-type built for the Black Mesa & Lake Powell Railroad's coal line. These were disappointing, however, and little better was achieved by the later and purpose-built General Electric E60-class units, which were limited to 85mph (137km/h). The solution was eventually found in Sweden, in the form of the ASEA Type Rc4 locomotive built by Budd and General Electric with electrical equipment supplied by the Swedish firm.

For its route linking New York and Boston, Amtrak inherited three examples of the Turbotrain built by United Aircraft

RIGHT

A Union Pacific E.9B No. 951, built between 1954 and 1963.

OPPOSITE,
ABOVE LEFT

Chesapeake & Ohio's 4-6-6 No. 490. Stainless steel casing converted it from 4-6-2 in 1946. On display at the Baltimore & Ohio Railroad Museum, Baltimore, Maryland.

BELOW LEFT

A Southern Pacific GN. E9.A of 2,400hp, built in 1954.

under the federal government's High Speed Ground Transportation programme of the late 1960s. These trains were based on advanced technology, but proved unequal to high-speed railroad operation, and the rising price of oil during the 1970s led to the three units' retirement. The Canadian National Railway Company had suffered similar problems with its nine-car turbo-trains, which had been introduced on the route linking Montreal and Toronto in 1969. These have often been removed from service, most seriously in 1979 after the destruction of three cars of one train in a fire, occasioned by the fracturing of a pipe, which then sprayed oil over the turbine in the power car. Amtrak once again turned to a European design in its effort to replace the Turbotrains. A two-year trial of French RTG units on the route between Chicago and St. Louis resulted in Amtrak's purchase of six sets from the French builder and a further seven manufactured under licence by Rohr.

The number of locomotives operating with American railroad companies fell steadily from 1929, firstly as a result of the depression of the 1930s and more recently because of the increased efficiency offered by the diesel locomotive. Since the mid-1960s, about 28,000 locomotives, almost all of them diesel units, have operated on U.S. railroads; with replacements running at between 1,000 and 1,500 units every year, the 1976 order book fell to less than 500 units.

CHAPTER EIGHT
PASSENGER SERVICES

The component of a train, other than the locomotive that hauls it, is the combination of cars that is hauled. The two main forms of car have traditionally been those for the carriage of passengers and of freight, and though the former had declined in importance by comparison with the latter since World War II, they were both of primary importance in the economics of railroad operation. Yet then as now, the lot of the passenger was not always a happy one. The passengers who embarked on the first service of the *DeWitt Clinton* on the Mohawk & Hudson Railroad in 1831 soon discovered the pitfalls of early railroad services: some were cast from their seats by the shock of starting, as the 3-ft (1-m) chains connecting the cars jolted taut, and most were soon having to stop their clothes from burning as masses of embers streamed onto them from the locomotive's smokestack. Any stop, such as that for water, caused the unbraked cars to shunt forward into the braking engine, and after

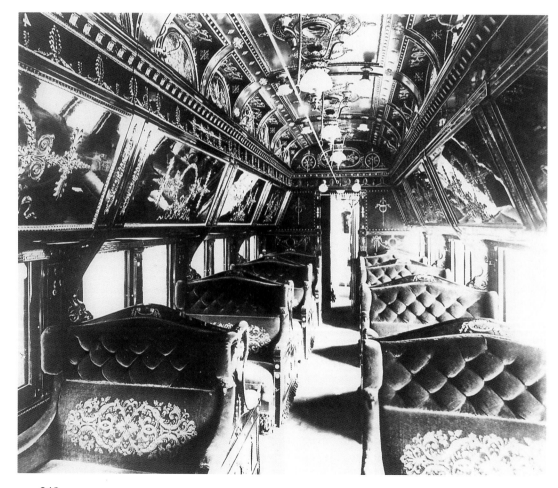

a drenching during the watering process, the passengers still with the train extemporized wooden buffers to jam between the cars. The journey then proceeded more smoothly, but ended with the passengers wearing very badly charred clothing.

Clearly there were some important improvements to be made before passenger travel by train could be considered endurable. Travel on the outside of a car clearly possessed ramifications altogether different from travel on an open horse-drawn wagon, and inside seating quickly became the norm. Stagecoach suspension was equally inadequate, and as early as three years after the *DeWitt Clinton*'s pioneering journey, Ross Winans patented a method to carry long cars on four-wheel bogies under their ends. This improved running on uneven track, and also facilitated the negotiation of curves. Once the use of independent bogies had made it feasible to build longer frames, the type of stagecoach bodies that had been used was replaced by the coach layout that is still standard. With the passengers now carried inside coaches, railroad transport was still dirty, noisy, uncomfortable and indeed dangerous. The quality of the ride was then enhanced by the development of cast-iron wheels that were more regular in shape than the hand-made wheels that had been standard up to that time. Spark-arresters helped to limit the damage done by embers from the smokestack, but a derailment was likely to cause a fire as

kerosene lamps and wood stoves, used to provide light and heat, were dislodged from their mountings.

Discomfort and danger were compounded by any number of inconveniences. For many years it was not possible to obtain through tickets covering more than one railroad, for example, and there were no facilities for baggage-handling or for onboard refreshment. Then the expansion of the railroads began to create competition for

Settling down for the night aboard an early U.S. train. (Illustrated Newspapers, February 1878.)

341

Centennial club car decorated in the 1890 motif which was in service on the Santa Fe streamliner Kansas City Chief.

trade, persuading the railroads to seek greater market share through the improvement of the passenger's lot; safety began to improve as the authorities began to consider the overall implications of railroad transport.

Much was achieved in the elimination of unnecessary dangers, especially in the quarter of a century following the end of the Civil War in 1865. Improvement of the trackwork through the introduction of heavier steel track combined with the appreciation that regular maintenance was required to reduce the possibility of sprung rails, which could pierce the bottoms of the carriages with dire results, and of derailments. The introduction of the Westinghouse vacuum brake and the Janney automatic coupler made starting and stopping more predictable. The replacement of stoves and kerosene lamps by steam-heating from the engine, and gas or electric lighting respectively, served to reduce the tendency toward fires. Outside the railroad train itself, improvement in signalling concepts and the spread of the telegraph also had their effect on reducing accident rates.

The development most liked by passengers, however, was probably the radical improvement in the design of the cars and their internal fittings. Here the name of George Pullman became synonymous with the best possible standards of comfort. Pullman was not the first man to create a sleeping car for the provision of night-time accommodation, the first recorded

sleeping car having appeared in the middle part of the 1830s on the Cumberland Valley Railroad in Pennsylvania. In this arrangement, stagecoach passengers arriving at Chambersburg late in the night were carried in an overnight train to Harrisburg for a connecting service to Philadelphia. But this and other early

attempts at creating effective overnight accommodation on trains were based on simple berths without bedding.

It was in 1853 that Pullman found himself on one such sleeper car on the route between Buffalo and Westfield. Apart from the obvious discomfort of the wooden berths, the most limiting factor in the provision of sleeping accommodation

The Modern Ship of the Plains, *a drawing from* Harper's Weekly *by R.F. Zogbaum, 1886.*

Interior of the Great Northern Pacific Railway's North Coast Limited *in April 1900 – the first train lit by electricity to cross the North-West.*

was, Pullman decided, the permanent attachment of the berths to the sides of the car, effectively preventing the car's profitable employment for daytime travel. A carpenter by training, Pullman decided to create a more versatile arrangement, and during 1858 converted two obsolete sleeping cars of the Chicago & Alton Railroad along the lines that his thoughts had taken him. Neither this first pair of conversions, nor a modest number of improved models that were effected slightly later, caused much of a stir among the members of the travelling public, but they gave Pullman the opportunity to test and evolve his ideas. After a short visit to the gold mining areas of Colorado, Pullman returned to Chicago with the determination to make the best possible car.

This emerged as the *Pioneer*, which marked a radical improvement in the type of comfort that passengers demanded, but was also much too large for service on the Chicago & Alton Railroad's system. Thus its fittings, valued at $20,000 rather than the standard $4,000 or so, and including carpets, brocade upholstery, polished wood, silvered oil lamps and gilded mirrors, served little practical purpose. In 1865, however, the body of President Lincoln arrived in Chicago on its way to Springfield; since the *Pioneer* was the obvious conveyance for the journey, the line was modified to allow the car's use. Later, the line between Detroit and Galena was similarly altered so that General Grant could travel home in the new car,

LEFT
'Old Number 9', a day coach remodelled by Leonard Seibert & George Pullman into the first Pullman sleeper. The lavish accommodation included ten sleeping car sections, a washstand, box-stove heater, oil lamps and plush seats. 1857.

345

Interior of one of the earliest Pullman cars operated on the Union Pacific Railroad.

*Interior of a purpose-built
Pullman-Standard carriage.*

Interior of the 'Frontier Shack' bar car on Union Pacific's City of Denver.

which was then placed in regular service on the Chicago & Alton Railroad's system. For the further exploitation of his concept, Pullman formed the Pullman Car Company in 1867, and his products soon became the very epitome of luxurious railroad travel.

Although the new company's first cars were sleeper units, Pullman's range soon developed. The hotel car, combining sleeping accommodation with a kitchen and portable tables, was a type manufactured for the Great Western Railway of Canada in 1867, and in 1888 Pullman made its first dining car for the Chicago & Alton Railroad. There followed beautifully appointed day cars, known as Palace Cars. Experience with these and other Pullman cars soon revealed that a connection between the individual cars would offer further attractions, and in 1887 there appeared Pullman's vestibuled car, which used steel springs to hold a steel-framed diaphragm over the platform at the end of one car against a similar arrangement on that of the next. This enabled passengers to cross in safety from car to car, and also made a major contribution to safety by reducing the tendency of the cars' platforms to ride over each other.

The introduction of the vestibuled car made it possible to create the so-called limited train with sleeping, dining, smoking, library, bathroom and even barber facilities. The limited train became very fashionable despite, or even because, of the higher charges that were

levied for the use of such a service.

It should not be imagined that Pullman merely built the cars bearing his name, leaving their operation to the railroads which bought them. Thus each car had its own Pullman attendant, carefully trained in the multitude of tasks involved in caring for the passengers. This concept lasted until 1947, when a case brought under American anti-trust legislation compelled the company to make a choice between building cars and operating them. The company opted for construction, passing responsibility for their operation to a new consortium, but then the current uncertainty about the future of American passenger travel led the company to abandon the construction of the cars themselves.

The success of the Pullman concept led to a mass of imitation. Many railroad operators built their own cars, while other concerns, including the Woodruff and Wagner companies, came into existence as the manufacturers and operators of this type of specialized passenger service. The Pullman name retained it hold, however, and over time the company created new and improved cars to satisfy changing requirements. In 1907 there appeared the first all-steel Pullman, and by this time the standard accommodation of a Pullman car included curtained seating sections which could be converted for night-time use with berths, a gentlemen's smoking compartment at one end of the car, and a ladies' drawing room at the other. Air-conditioning was a feature that became

LEFT
Poster advertising the luxury of Pullman Hotel Cars on the Chicago & North-Western Railway in the late 1800s.

Restaurant service in Baltimore & Ohio's Colonial dining car Mount Vernon.

increasingly standard from the late 1920s, and in the 1930s the roomette was introduced to replace the curtained alcoves with individual compartments that combined day seating, folding berths and toilet facilities. At first, each car was outfitted with 18 roomettes, but the staggering of the position of the floors and the arranging of one bed to slide underneath the higher floor, and the bed in the next compartment to fold against the wall, allowed each car to be outfitted with 24 individual roomettes.

A large part of the discomfort associated with early rail journeys over any but the shortest routes was their very length. The introduction of the Pullman and similar cars for the wealthier passengers, and of generally more comfortable accommodation in the standard cars for the less wealthy, certainly went a long way to improve the lot of the longer-distance traveller, but clearly a shorter travelling time also had its part to play. Thus the improvement in accommodation was paralleled by an increase in the average speed of railroad journeys. Despite the fact that trains averaged about 40mph (64km/h) and inappropriately sported names such as *Thunderbolt*, those involved in long-distance travel still had to make frequent changes: even in highly industrialized and technically advanced New York, large numbers of train journeys started with a ferry trip across the Hudson, since only the New York Central Railroad, with its Grand Central Station, had a terminus in

Interior of a Santa Fe Pullman coach used in the 1930s.

In the bar of the City of Los Angeles *in the 1940s.*

the city; the only other railroad allowed to operate from this was the New York, New Haven & Hartford Railroad. This situation was improved only in 1910, when the Pennsylvania Railroad opened its own station on Manhattan Island. One consequence of this move was to intensify competition on the route from New York to Chicago, which in the 1890s had as many as 44 services every day.

The fact that the different operators worked over different routes when connecting the same pairs of cities inevitably meant that there were major differences in journey times, and before World War I the railroads operating services between New York and Chicago came to an agreement that 28 hours would became standard for the journey. Since the distances involved ranged from the Pennsylvania Railroad's 903 miles (1453km) to the Erie Railroad's 996 miles (1603km), it was also decided that $1 would be added to fares for each hour that any service subtracted from the standard time. The leading lights on the New York and Chicago run were the Pennsylvania and the New York Central Railroads, which operated their prestige trains, the *Broadway Limited* and the *Twentieth Century Limited* respectively, between the two cities in 18 hours, increased to 20 hours after World War I; given the fact that the availability of Pullman cars on these two services was limited, there was scope for a very large difference in price between the slowest and least well equipped services and their

Dinner on board the Super Chief, *Santa Fe Railway's de luxe Chicago to Los Angeles streamliner.*

Interior of the observation car of the Santa Fe Super Chief.

A well-appointed bedroom suite on a Santa Fe streamliner.

altogether faster and better equipped counterparts.

In the period of affluence during the 1920s, the railroads placed emphasis on service, but during this decade the motor car became steadily a more important rival to the train, causing speed to assume a more important position in the thinking of the railroads. This trend led to the introduction, during the 1930s, of the streamliners, which were high-speed trains that attracted very considerable publicity from their spectacular looks and high performance, and were a major weapon in the railroads' struggle to retain traffic at a time when this was being degraded by the period's economic depression and the growing popularity of private transport.

The first streamliner was introduced by the Union Pacific Railroad, using Pullman-built aluminium cars and an early diesel locomotive. This locomotive entered service only after a demonstration tour as the *City of Salina*, and during 1934 recorded speeds of up to 110mph (177km/h) with only 400hp (298kW), in the process showing its potential for the combination of great operational economy, high speed, and impressive appearance.

Clearly an impressive name would catch on and retain the interest and even the enthusiasm of the public. One of the first railroads to operate streamliner services, the Chicago, Burlington & Quincy Railroad started the trend in 1934 with its *Zephyr* services. The initial *Zephyr*

OPPOSITE
Dining Car on the Super Chief *in 1957.*

LEFT
The combined Super Chief *and* El Capitan *speed eastwards in northern Arizona, past a typical Navajo hogan with sheep and a woman weaving.*

Cocktail lounge on the Santa Fe Super Chief.

Sleeping compartment aboard the Santa Fe Super Chief.

OPPOSITE
Railroads operating in many parts of the U.S.A., and especially in the western regions, can provide their passengers with the most magnificent views. This is the Animas Canyon seen from a service of the Denver & Rio Grande Western Railroad.

LEFT
Silverton: the end of the line for Denver & Rio Grande locomotive No. 476.

The Auto-Train concept offered the advantages of easy and stress-free movement over long distances, with the passengers' own cars available at the destination. However, this facility was only short-lived as the growth of mass air transport and the ready availability of rental cars offered still greater advantages.

was a three-car train built by Budd of Philadelphia and using an early 600-hp (447.5-kW) Electromotive diesel engine. The *Zephyr*'s first service linked Lincoln, Nebraska, and Kansas City via Omaha, and passenger reaction was sufficiently encouraging for the railroad to inaugurate this type of service on other routes.

Not all of the new streamliners were diesel-powered operations. In 1935, for example, the Milwaukee Road began its *Hiawatha* services with steam locomotives fitted with moderately efficient and visually stunning streamlined 'overcoats'. The *Hiawatha* service was initially operated on the very competitive route between Chicago and Minneapolis and St. Paul, but was then extended to include runs north to the shore of Lake Superior and west to Omaha, Sioux Falls and across the continent, by means of the *Olympian Hiawatha*, to Spokane in Washington state. Other western long-distance streamliners included such famous trains as the Atchison, Topeka & Santa Fe Railroad's *Super Chief*, which was launched in 1937 with diesel locomotion and Pullman coaches on the vast route linking Chicago and Los Angeles, and the Union Pacific Railroad's *City of Los Angeles*, *City of Portland* and *City of San Francisco* that served the cities for which they were named.

One exception to the general rule of the streamliners' marketing ploy of the highest speed and the finest accommodation came after World War II, the period in which the train was facing

new competition from the airlines on the longer routes. Having pioneered the high-speed concept in the 1930s, the Chicago, Burlington & Quincy Railroad in 1949 introduced the domeliner, in the form of the *California Zephyr* whose coaches included domed observation cars built by Budd for this specific application and

intended to offer an extra incentive by providing the traveller with the best possible views of the vistas of the Far West. The lead of the Chicago, Burlington & Quincy Railroad was followed by a number of other operators, including the Canadian Pacific Railway. In Canada, the transcontinental railroads were exactly

Dining car of the Auto-Train.

Amtrak's double-deck coaches on the Southwest Limited *in the late 1970s.*

maintained its *Southern Crescent* in service between Washington and New Orleans, with a through sleeping car service to Los Angeles; but there was not enough demand to warrant the retention of many other services. Some operations were accorded new names, however. One of the most celebrated of the old streamliners was the Southern Pacific Railroad's *Coast Daylight* between Los Angeles and San Francisco, and this was turned into the *Coast Starlight*, extended along most of the U.S.A.'s western seaboard between Seattle and Los Angeles. The *Hiawatha* also survives as the *North Coast Hiawatha*.

The great majority of surviving railroads now operate only freight services, and passenger trains run on only a very small minority of the main-line tracks they once dominated. Even where passenger services are still operated, the journey times are considerably longer than those typical of the 1930s and 1950s in open acceptance of the fact that any attempt to rival air transport over long distances is clearly not possible; the fact is that much of the American railroad system is no longer capable of handling high-speed services without major overhauls and updatings of track and associated equipment.

There were still a number of innovative and specialized services to come, however, the latter offering a facility impossible or at least very difficult with any other form of transport. Typical of these specialized service operations was the Auto-Train Corporation, formed

that, and from the 1880s the Canadian Pacific Railway and later the Canadian National Railway Company have operated services right through from Montreal and Vancouver. In 1955 the Canadian Pacific Railway introduced its own domecar train for the aptly named *Canadian* service. Declining traffic hit the Canadian services as much as it affected American services in later years. The Canadian National Railway Company's *Dominion* transcontinental service was withdrawn in 1965, and from 1978 the

establishment of the national VIA Rail passenger service operation led to the combination of the surviving *Canadian* and Canadian National Railway's *Super Continental* services over much of the transcontinental route between Sudbury and Winnipeg.

The establishment of Amtrak heralded the end of many of the famous old names in the U.S.A. The Denver & Rio Grande Western Railroad continued to operate its *Rio Grande Zephyr* between Denver and Salt Lake City, and Southern Railroad

Amtrak's Union Station, Los Angeles.

PASSENGER SERVICES

in 1969 after studies undertaken by the Ford Motor Company and agencies of the federal government had concurred that there was potential for profitable implementation of a motor car ferry operation. The passengers had the comforts of long-distance train transport as well as the convenience of taking their automobiles with them. Auto-Train bought sleeping cars and day coaches from a variety of railroads, together with auto-carrying cars from the Canadian National Railway Company and new locomotives from General Electric, and began its service in 1971 on the tracks of

the Seaboard Coast Line and the Richmond, Fredericksburg & Potomac Railroad between Lorton in Virginia and Sanford in Florida. The popularity of the holiday route to Florida enabled Auto-Train to show a healthy operating profit by the mid-1970s. A second service between Louisville and Sanford, operated in conjunction with Amtrak, was discontinued in 1977. Another innovatory service was introduced by Auto-Train in collaboration with Eastern Airlines, and allowed tourists to fly to Florida and have their automobiles delivered by train.

It should be noted that while prestige

services have inevitably attracted the highest levels of attention, such services have always been in the minority of the relevant railroads' passenger operations. During the later part of the 19th century, for example, the railroads operated large numbers of special immigrant trains for the movement of families newly arrived on the eastern seaboard to the new lands they were going to settle in the West. Indeed, several of the transcontinental lines, mainly those operating in or into the north-western parts of the U.S.A., employed agents in Europe to advertise the attractions of the new country and arrange passage for the resulting flow of emigrants. The conditions on many of the trains that met the new arrivals were poor: the sleeping cars had only wooden benches along their sides as berths, and the cars were kept as open as possible so that that they could be easily hosed down after they had discharged their passengers.

At the other end of the price and facility scale there were the luxurious private saloon cars for the use of wealthy travellers. Built to the individual's particular specification and limited only by the dimensions and the owner's ability to pay, these cars represented the last word in luxury. Several companies undertook such work, and the Pullman company manufactured some 450 coaches for private customers before the great crash of 1929 ended this type of extravagance: Pullman's prices ranged from a minimum of $50,000 to a maximum of $350,000.

One of the most important and successful rapid-transit developments in recent years has been the BART (Bay Area Rapid Transport) system, which provides clean, affordable and fast services for local commuters, in the process removing a certain amount of car traffic from the overloaded road network.

Night passenger services such as this, seen in progress through Plainfield, New Jersey, are now something of a rarity except for short-distance commuter routes.

CHAPTER NINE
FREIGHT MOVEMENT

Other than the movement of passengers, the other function of the train is the movement of freight, and this type of operation in fact preceded not only the concept of passenger transport but also of the locomotive itself, in even its most primitive steam-powered form. In its very earliest days, the railway was employed to facilitate the handling of heavy loads, initially in quarries and mines. In the U.S.A. it was the commercial attractions of collecting the agricultural produce of the country's westward expansion that first encouraged railroad operators to extend their tracks from the east coast toward the great rivers of the interior. These operators at first planned to run their railroads in much the same way as the operators of toll roads and canals: the operator would provide the tracks, and payment of the requisite fee would allow anyone to haul their own vehicles over them. The concept almost immediately proved ineffective, and the operators took complete control of all elements of the

OPPOSITE
A Currier & Ives lithograph of the Niagara suspension bridge between the U.S.A. and Canada. 1856.

LEFT
Shunting a Santa Fe Railroad Ten-pack TOFC (trailer-on-flatcar) unit at the Kansas City yards in the late 1970s.

OPPOSITE
A Boston & Maine unit coal train serving the Public Service Company's Bow, New Hampshire power plant from the West Virginia coalfields. Here the line-up at Bow is headed by a GP38-2- class diesel locomotive (No. 207).

LEFT
A Union Pacific freight train, headed by the 5,000-hp EMD DD35 diesel locomotive No. 80, crosses the John Day bridge at the Columbia river gorge.

OPPOSITE
A six-locomotive combination hauls a 109-coal-hopper train out of Trinidad, southern Colorado. Santa Fe SD40-2 locos 5205 and 5211 lead four Burlington Northern locos, 5026 (C30-7), 7190 (SD40-2), 5813 (U30C) and 5377 (U30C). Note tail end of train crossing in the background.

LEFT
Santa Fe Railroad's TOFC train near Victorville, California, en route to Chicago in the late 1970s.

movement. This included the provision of the locomotives; right types of car; depots where goods could be delivered, loaded, unloaded and collected; and the administrative system that made the whole system workable. These are the basic elements that still characterize railroad freight operations.

The same type of locomotives were initially used for both passenger and freight services, but it soon became clear that each type of operation could best be handled by locomotives designed and built for that task. Passenger services required the use of locomotives optimized for speed rather than power as the loads were comparatively light, while freight services needed locomotives optimized for power rather than speed as the loads were heavier. In practical terms, this led to the development of the freight locomotive with driving wheels that were more numerous but smaller in diameter than those of locomotives optimized for the movement of passengers.

With speed a relatively insignificant factor in freight operations, except when perishable agricultural produce was involved, the primary requirement in freight operations became the movement

of the maximum possible quantity of freight in each train. Some notably enormous steam locomotives were created and manufactured specifically to work vast freight trains, but the introduction of the diesel engine was a major milestone in freight operations, for at last it was possible to locate the motive power away from a single point. During the period of steam locomotion, when it had generally been impossible to locate the power

anywhere but at the head or tail of the string of freight cars, the size of the freight train was limited by the load that could be supported by the couplings. Then the advent of the diesel-engined power unit opened the way for remote control of a number of power units, making it possible for slave locomotives to be located at intervals along the train and so spread the load and balance the power that had to be exerted.

An earlier breakthrough in the control of long trains was the introduction of the quick-acting airbrake. At first, freight cars were individually braked, which required the brakeman to move along the roofs of the cars to reach the wheels by which the brakes were controlled: this was a slow and inefficient system, and one fraught with danger to brakemen, many of whom were killed. What was needed was a system that allowed the brakes to be

OPPOSITE
Baltimore & Ohio Railroad's 100-ton coal hopper, built by Pullman-Standard in 1975.

LEFT
Chicago & North Western Railroad's SD45 on a unit coal train.

RIGHT
*Atchison, Topeka & Santa Fe
SD24 2,400-hp diesels.*

OPPOSITE
*A Santa Fe Safe-Pak car
transporter being loaded.*

controlled from a single point in the locomotive, making it feasible for the brakes in every car to be applied simultaneously. By the 1870s the Westinghouse type of airbrake, offering this capability, was entering large-scale service in passenger trains. The introduction of Westinghouse airbrakes in freight trains, especially those of greater length, was initially less successful as the time required for the braking force to be transmitted along the full length of the train could lead to severe shocks in the rearmost cars. By the mid-1880s a version of the Westinghouse airbrake system with the capacity for quicker action had been developed, and its use made it possible for long trains to be stopped without significant delay or shocks.

The adoption of a braking system that was universal on American railroads was important for a number of reasons, of which the most important was probably the growth of through-traffic, as this led to the spread of cars belonging to different railroad operators all over the rail network. This tendency was also a direct reflection of the growth of freight operations' size and importance. It also required the railroads to create car-accounting departments whose sole task was to keep track of the location of every one of the railroad's cars: railroads were charged on a daily basis for the use of other companies' cars, so the car-accounting department was a vital tool in each railroads' operations to ensure that the right rentals were charged for their

OPPOSITE and LEFT
Remoter areas rich in raw materials required by the great industries of the U.S.A. generate a need for a reliable bulk transport capability. These photographs of services near Provo, Utah, by the Utah Railway, reveal the nature of the task.

OPPOSITE and LEFT
There may be something incongruous about the movement of a modern freight service, such as these by the Santa Fe Railroad in the Cajon area of the western USA, in country that is more familiar from Western movies set in the 19th century; but heavy freight services of this nature are very much a part of the industrial and commercial lifeblood of the U.S.A.

FREIGHT MOVEMENT

BELOW
Union Pacific's EMD SD40-2 3,000-hp diesel locomotive No. 3175, heads the first train through the Aspen Tunnel.

OPPOSITE
An eastbound Super Continental *train standing in Jasper station, Alberta.*

own cars, and that other operators' empty cars were returned as rapidly as possible.

Car-accounting is still a vital aspect of freight operations, but is now handled on an altogether more sophisticated basis by systems such as the Southern Pacific Railroad's Total Operations Processing System. This is a computer-based system that is updated on a constant basis with data about every element of the railroad's operation. This means that within seconds it can be established exactly where, on the operator's 13,500 miles (21725km) of track, any one of its 120,000

cars is located. This allows the Southern Pacific Railroad's management to keep a close eye on the efficient use of car resources and provide customers with precise data on the progress of their loads.

Over the years there has inevitably developed an increasing level of specialization in the cars used for freight transport. In the early days of freight transport by rail, the three most common types were the flatcar, the boxcar and the coal car, and cars of these types are still in widespread service. However, the cars of

these three basic types are the results of constant improvement. Other types of car now in large-scale use include the refrigerated car for the movement of perishable farm produce, and an ever-enlarging number of role-specialized cars such as three-deck automobile carriers and tank cars for the carriage of liquid loads. Two other very important types of car for freight purposes are those designed for the carriage of standard containers, and those employed for 'piggyback' service, a system in which truck trailers are loaded complete with their loads onto a flatcar to minimize transfer time between road and rail at transhipment points. In recent years, piggyback traffic has witnessed the greatest growth of any aspect of freight operations.

Coal has long been carried in larger quantities than any other type of freight load by North American railroads. The whole process is now automated to a high degree, especially by operators such as the Norfolk & Western Railroad, which delivers huge weights of coal from mining areas of Kentucky and West Virginia for domestic use in the industrial cities, mainly in the area to the south of the Great Lakes, and for export sales via its port facilities at Lamberts Point on Chesapeake Bay. The Norfolk & Western Railroad's operation handles more than 2 million tons of coal each month at Lamberts Point, where there is a mass of advanced equipment ranging from infra-red thawing sheds, where the coal is

OPPOSITE

Like the Santa Fe Railroad, the Southern Pacific Railroad operates in regions of some inhospitality in the western part of the U.S.A.

LEFT

In less hospitable parts of the U.S.A. it makes sense to build roads for wheeled vehicles and tracks for trains alongside each other to share the smallest available gradients and largest-radius curves. This is a freight service of the Santa Fe Railroad near Cajon.

Three SD50 locomotives, produced by General Motor's Electromotive Division at La Grange, Illinois, power Kansas City Southern freight. EMD locomotives comprise 100 per cent of the KCS fleet.

defrosted if it has become frozen in the course of its journey from the mountain mining districts, to radar speed measuring, automatic weight recording and blending, and rotary dumpers. These last can each handle 252 cars per hour, the process turning the car through 165 degrees so that the coal pours out and the car is righted once more.

A similar undertaking, and one performed under somewhat more difficult conditions, is that of CP Rail in Canada. This operator had ten specialized trains that every year move 8 million tons of coal from the mining area near Crowsnest Pass in the Rocky Mountains to a new port at Roberts Bank, near Vancouver, for shipment across the Pacific Ocean to Japan. The movement of coal that is required in this process is based on continuous loading and rotary dumping, but the most difficult element of the whole programme is the movement of trains between the mountains and the coast. The ten trains are worked as permanent units, with 95 cars each carrying 115 tons of coal. The nature of the line means that for some stages of each train's trip, up to 11 locomotives, each delivering 3,000hp (2237kW), are used under the control of a computer to ensure the correct balancing of the power and traction so that the train does not break down under the application of uneven loads.

Unit trains of this type are notably cost-effective as far as operators are concerned, for they avoid all need for the operator to make up trains with loads

from different companies for delivery to different destinations along and sometimes off the route to be travelled. This need to make up trains became inevitable after railroad routes began to meet and thereby open the way for the transhipments of loads, often from the lines of one operator to those of another. This often led to considerable delays in the completion of many loads, and in an effort to overcome this problem there appeared a number of fast freight lines in the course of the 19th century. Established by agreements between the groups of railroads primarily involved or between separate operators, the fast freight lines contracted with shippers to undertake the through shipment of their loads between different railroads.

After World War I, the task of handling individual cars and making up trains was facilitated by the automation of the classification yards where these tasks were handled. One of the first yards of this more modern type was the Markham Yard of the Illinois Central Railroad, just south of Chicago. The factor whose development allowed the introduction of large-scale automation was the remote-controlled retarder used in concert with power-operated switches and a hump to enable all the yard's activities to be controlled from a central tower with good all-round fields of vision. In the first period of North American railroad operations, the movement of all the cars in a yard was undertaken by individual switching of the engines to move them

LEFT
Canadian Pacific Railway's huge marshalling yard at Alyth, Calgary, Alberta.

BELOW LEFT
These 44 new diesel locomotives were delivered to Consolidated Rail Corporation as part of a 217-locomotive, $113-million order received in 1978. With completion of this order, Conrail has more than 4,500 diesel locomotives in its fleet, nearly 400 of which have been acquired new since Conrail began operations on 1 April 1976.

OPPOSITE
This is a freight service of the Union Pacific Railroad near Santa Cruz, and was photographed in April 1999.

LEFT
This multiple-headed freight service of the Union Pacific Railroad is caught by the camera in the somewhat inappropriately named Meadow Valley region.

OPPOSITE

An eastbound Southern Pacific freight of 123 bogies, plus caboose, heads over the Cajon Pass summit in the San Gabriel mountains, California, hauled by three SD45-2 locomotives, Nos. 9315, 9253, 9390, and SD40R locomotive No. 7300. The last, No. 7300, is a rebuild of an SD40 unit, with updated electrics from the SD40-2.

LEFT

Utility, measured in terms of reliability and cost-efficiency, is the hallmark of the locomotive intended for freight-hauling duties. This is a locomotive of this type from the fleet of the Southern Pacific Railroad.

into the siding where their train was being made up. This was a slow and laborious system that was greatly simplified in the 1880s by the introduction of humps, or artificial mounds, over which all the cars could be pushed in turn and then coasted downhill, with the appropriate switch setting, to their allotted sidings. The system was further speeded by the introduction of power-operated switches,

but reached its definitive form with the installation of retarders, which are track-side beams that can be operated to grip the wheels of passing cars and thereby slow them, to allow full control of all the yard's activities from a central location.

The Markham Yard opened in 1926, and at that time the northbound classification section had 121 retarders and 69 pairs of switches feeding 67 tracks, with

five towers to supervise operations. The advent of computerized control systems has further enhanced this already improved concept by making possible completely centralized control. Such a facility is CP Rail's Alyth Yard at Calgary where, with the exception of the uncoupling of the cars as they pass over the hump, the entire operation is controlled by a central computer. Further

capability is provided to systems of this sort by the use of automatic car identification, ensuring that the right car is sent to the correct siding: the label marking on the side of each car is read by a photoelectric scanner so that the type of car, its owner and its individual identification can be established with precision. Extended in scope by the location of other photoelectric scanners at key points on the main lines, this is the system that makes it possible for

computerized central systems, such as the Southern Pacific Railroad's TOPS, to 'know' the exact position of every car in the system.

The effective use of the retarder is based necessarily on a nice calculation of a number of factors, including the car's type, whether or not the car is loaded, the car's degree of freedom in running, the strength and direction of the wind, and the route to the individual siding. The integration of all these factors is necessary

for assessment of the amount of pressure each pair of retarders exerts on the wheels to make certain that the car neither ceases to move before reaching the steadily varying numbers of other cars already at a halt in the siding, nor crashes into them.

It was the very number of the variable factors, and the need for human crews to keep the cars under observation right through the shunting process, that demanded the use of several control towers in each major yard, until the

OPPOSITE
*Delaware & Hudson GP39-2
No. 7401 runs a Maine
Central Railroad freight
along the bank of the
Penobscot river into Bangor,
Maine, from the north. Both
railroads, along with the
Boston & Maine are now
part of the Guildford
Transportation Industries.*

LEFT
*Freight-hauling services are
the key to the continued
existence of major operators
such as the Denver & Rio
Grande Western Railroad.*

advent of the computer made it feasible to automate virtually the whole of the process and thereby permit a reduction in the number of control towers to one. Such automation is expensive in capital terms to establish, but allows significant savings once it has entered service. Manpower can be reduced, and the swifter and more accurate classification of trains makes for much more efficient use of the railroad's assets: the Alyth Yard, for example, has the space for 5,200 standing cars, and can handle the movement of 3,000 cars every day.

Automation to a very high degree makes the best possible economic sense in an operation that is dedicated to a single high-volume task. Typical of this type of operation is the handling of coal in bulk, and fully automated systems associated with this task include the Norfolk & Western Railroad's traffic to Lamberts Point and the Chesapeake & Ohio Railroad's nearby system, delivering coal to Newport News. The Norfolk & Western Railroad's coal is classified into almost 1,000 different categories, and the blend specified by a particular customer is produced by an automated system, which ensures the speed and ratio of coal falling from bins onto conveyor belts to yield exactly the desired combination of sizes or grades. The right blend and quantity of coal is then transported out to the relevant ship by huge loading towers with 120-ft (36.6-m) extendable booms that drop the coal in the ship's hold.

In the normal classification yards,

where there is a mixture in the types of freight handled, there are wider-ranging systems such as the automatic weighing of cars as they pass over the hump; moreover, more capable computerized systems allow the establishment not only of the total weight but also the loading on each axle, the latter allowing unbalanced loads to be redistributed so that they cause no problems in high-speed running.

As noted above, one of the aspects of freight that offers the railroad operator the optimum conditions for a useful profit is the operation of unit trains, in which all the cars are bound for the same destination. It was for the optimization of this process that the Atchison, Topeka & Santa Fe Railroad constructed its huge classification yard at Barstow in California. Here, traffic previously assembled at yards in other parts of California is brought together, before being hauled to the east. The effective use of the yard's facilities allows the concentration, in time and space, of cars that can then be classified by destination and shunted accordingly to allow more timely assembly of trains. A similar but not so capable yard is located at Kansas City for the classification of westbound freight, but intermediate traffic is hauled to Barstow in mixed freights and then made up into trains for the various destination points in California.

Once a train had left the yard, there must be continued control of its movement for two primary reasons: the arrival of the train at its destination at the

right time, and the control of all the movements in a given area to ensure that there are no collisions. The first effective way in which this task was accomplished in the 19th century, was by means of the newly created telegraph system to issue train orders. Linked by telegraph to station operators, the central despatcher sent orders governing the movements of all the trains on the line, and these orders were then written out and passed to the engineer and conductor of every applicable train. This system ensured that each engineer was given his instructions, told of all other traffic on the line, informed of the priority accorded to the various trains, and all other relevant details. The system still exists in some parts, and is of particular importance when any train must progress along a long stretch of single-track line with passing sections that trains moving in opposite directions must reach at the same time: thus the engineer might be instructed to move to a specified passing point, with a loop in the track allowing him to pull off the main line and wait until the other train has passed before continuing. The engineer of the other train would have been told to move off but also warned of the first train and told where to expect to find it waiting in its loop. If the sidelined train was not in its appointed place, the train with the right of way would stop and telegraph the despatcher by means of a portable telegraph machine that could be tapped into the line at the side of the track. So important was the telegraph to

successful and safe operation of the railroads that it was one of the fundamental rules that no train should depart without a telegrapher.

Improvement with the passage of time led to the introduction of block signalling for sections of any line where there was heavy traffic. This allowed the control of all the trains on that section by means of semaphore or coloured light signals. These were operated from a central control point with the levers for setting the switches, and was later enhanced by an interlock arrangement between signals and switches: mechanically connecting all the controls, the arrangement ensured that a signal could not be set unless the individual switches were in the appropriate position for the instruction given. Block signalling is impractical for many parts of a large railroad network, and here the modern system is centralized train control. This was developed during the 1920s, and places the whole section of line under the despatcher's direct control, with points and signals set by electrically actuated control. The lag in time inherent in the transmission and execution of the command signals is then reduced by the replacement of the original electro-mechanical controls by electronic systems, and the despatcher's control panels have also been enhanced so that a continuous indication of any train's movement is represented by coloured lights. Radio equipment in the engineer's cab provides an additional means of control from and communication with the control centre,

and the cab has also been fitted with a signalling system to provide a continuous picture of the line yet to be covered, this replacing the older system that provided only limited indications from intermittent trackside signals.

Such centralization reflects the overall pattern of the operations of American railroads. Since their first days, the railroads have always been subject to a vibrant pattern of financial give-and-take characterized by a gradual but steady movement toward consolidation. The process of mergers and acquisitions has gradually created a smaller number of larger railroad operators, and the result of modern mergers have national rather than regional or state implications. Two of the more recent alterations in the status quo of American railroad operations have been the mergers of the Chessie and Family Lines systems to form the CSX Corporation with 26,600 miles (42810km) of railroad, and of the Burlington Northern and Frisco systems to bring 27,300 miles (43935km) of railroad under one management. The pattern inevitably continues as surviving railroads look for economies that can often be found only in operations on a grand scale.

The Norfolk & Western Railroad, for example, resulted from a series of mergers and acquisitions. In 1959 it combined with the nearby Virginian Railway, and in 1964 it absorbed the Wabash & Nickel Plate as well as three smaller railroads. The first merger consolidated the operator's position as a leading coal carrier, while the

second extended its activities into areas such as automobile parts and also enlarged its operating area into the grain-producing areas of Kansas and Nebraska, added a main line into Canada, and provided it with access to many important cities.

The pattern of mergers is likely to be accelerated by the 1980 Staggers Rail Act. This changed the conditions under which the Interstate Commerce Commission can approve railroad mergers, but also relaxed the regulations for the abandonment of lines and lifted many of the regulations governing freight rates.

American railroads carry more than 900 billion ton-miles of freight each year: this has been translated as the carriage of some 1.5 million tons of freight moved 600 miles (965km). Coal is still the single most important type of freight, but the pattern of freight is subject, like all other economic factors in a free state, to market forces that may alter this situation. One of the most significant areas of growth has been piggyback container traffic, as noted above, and this is second only to coal in the lives of the railroads. The growth of

ABOVE
Locomotive No. 26 of the Union Pacific Railroad.

OPPOSITE
Pennsylvania Railroad EMD F7s on westbound freight climbing Horseshoe Curve, Altoona.

importance in the market for piggyback transport has led many operators to take an innovatory look at their operations in the hope of boosting their share of this traffic, which is still very small by comparison with that of road haulers. The most obvious area in which improvement can be effected is that of speed. One operator which has made a determined effort to compete with road transport in terms of speed is the Illinois Central Gulf Railroad. This railroad's Slingshot high-speed container service links Chicago and St. Louis with delivery of the 300-mile (485km) distance in just 7 hours.

Another step toward more efficient container handling is the Ten-Pack concept of the Atchison, Topeka & Santa Fe Railroad. The system is based on the use of specially designed container cars with only a skeleton bed to support the trailer's lower structural frame, and the cars are also very low to the track to reduce drag. The combination of lower weight and reduced drag makes possible significant fuel savings by 100-car sets on the long haul between Chicago and Los Angeles.

Another form of the integration of road and rail transport is the roadrailer, with two types of running gear to allow it to operate on roads and rails. After the failure of a pioneering attempt on this concept in the first part of the 1960s, the Chesapeake & Ohio Railroad revived the concept in the late 1970s with a roadrailer incorporating running gear that can be switched between its two modes in less than 3 minutes, and has been hauled at

more than 100mph (160km/h) in 75-car trains.

It should be noted, though, that while some aspects of railroad freight operations have increased in volume and financial importance, others have declined to greater or lesser extents. One of the most significant of these is the movement of cattle, which was one of the primary reasons for the extension of the railroads into the region of Kansas, where cities such as Abilene and Dodge City provided the points at which cattle herded from Texas were gathered for railroad movement to the great stock yards of Kansas City and Chicago. Speed of movement is clearly important in the transport of live animals, and here the Chicago, Burlington & Quincy Railroad was among the leaders with average speeds of nearly 50mph (80km/h). In the early 1960s, as the railroad movement of live cattle was beginning its decline, trains regularly covered the distance from Denver in Colorado to Chicago in less than 30 hours with double-deck stock cars. The Chicago, Burlington & Quincy Railroad also undertook trials of special livestock containers that could be carried on ordinary flatcars so that it would not need to buy and maintain the special stock cars that were used for only a small part of the year. By this time, though, the meat-packing companies were moving their facilities nearer to the cattle-producing area, and the practice of moving large numbers of cattle by railroad had effectively disappeared.

The same has happened to the railroad movement of mail. The mail was first carried by trains in 1838 on a regular basis following the decision of the Congress that all railroads should be post carriers, although some mail service had been operated before this. From 1838 onward, the movement of mail by the railroads grew steadily in capability and volume. Whereas the first mail had been moved in locked compartments, from the 1860s more effective use was made of the concept after the railroad had reached St. Joseph and the jumping-off point for the Pony Express service for mail deliveries to California. Following the suggestion of a member of the U.S. Postal Service in St. Joseph, it was decided that mail would be sorted on board the train to avoid the delay inherent in sorting before being loaded onto the train. It August 1864, therefore, mail sorting facilities, as already used in Canada and therefore modelled on the British pattern, were pioneered by the Hannibal & St. Joseph Railroad. Post office cars then became standard on many of the faster railroad services, the teams in these cars sorting the mail for the various points on the route. As the volume of mail increased, dedicated mail trains were operated. Like the cattle trains, though, mail trains have become a thing of the past.

OPPOSITE
Two Seaboard Systems B36-8 locomotives, Nos. 5843 and 5867, plus three U18B locos, wait in Tampa yard, Florida, with a northbound freight of car transporters and trailers.

OPPOSITE
This Southern Pacific Railroad freight service has been caught on camera in the region of Tehachapi, California.

LEFT
The carriage of a superimposed pair of containers on a single flatcar, as seen on this freight service of the SSW near Benson, maximizes capacity without adding to the overall length of the train.

CHAPTER TEN

LIGHT RAIL & RAPID TRANSIT SYSTEMS

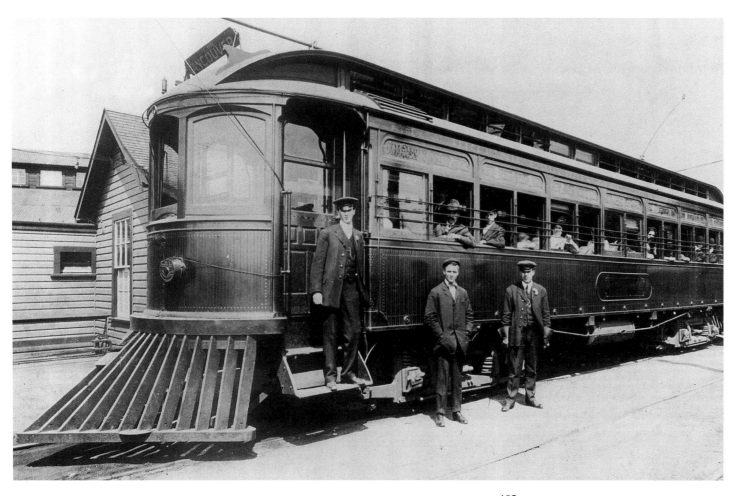

Almost as soon as the spread of the railroads had created the framework on which vast commercial and industrial expansion could flourish in American cities, this expansion began to add another, larger dimension to railroad operations. So while the development of the railroads had spurred the growth of cities, the growth of cities now led to the further development of the railroads. This expansion provided the means for the inhabitants of nearby towns to travel to and from work in newly established factories and businesses. These towns were gradually subsumed by the cities they supported to become suburbs, and railroad services spread ever further. At an early point in this process of local growth, commuter traffic became a specialized form of railroad transport in its own right, characterized by its own types of rolling stock and, inevitably, its own operational problems.

In the decades following the end of the Civil War, railroads spawned the development of the suburbs. Industry and the railroads were dependent on each other: industry could increase only on the basis of rail transport, and the growth of industry and the commerce it supported provided the traffic the railroads needed. The suburbs had a vital part to play in this process of mutual growth, providing both the workforce to operate industry and commerce and the market for their products. Large and regular traffic over the same routes seemed an ideal form of business to railroad planners. Even before the end of the 19th century, however, it had become clear that suburban services would be increasingly difficult as commuter traffic required large amounts of rolling stock and locomotives, sophisticated organization and great efficiency, but would operate for only a few hours each day. Trains had to be run in both directions, but were filled only in one direction at a time, namely into the cities at the start of the working day and out to the suburbs at its end. Maximization of passenger loads required the introduction of purpose-built coaches with minimal facilities, and these were of no use for other purposes.

This was only the start of the railroads' problems, for the situation became worse as time passed. During the 1920s there began to develop serious competition from the private motor car, the 1930s saw a great economic depression, and World War II was followed by a further significant diminution of passenger traffic. By the 1960s, commuter operations were

at crisis point. The profits of commuter operations were at best small, and this had meant that for some considerable time little had been achieved in the modernization of equipment, and now any attempt seemed only to exacerbate matters: increases in fares led to further loss of passengers, and increases in demand for uneconomic services entailed greater losses for the railroads. Demand for increased passenger capacity was prompted by increased road congestion in the 1960s, but commuter needs were still concentrated in rush hour periods when

services were already under pressure, and was accompanied by continuing decline in custom during the rest of the week.

Yet it was also recognized that commuter services were essential to the continued life of cities. Public transport was a necessity, and it was now understood that it could be provided only with the aid of large quantities of public money. The current pattern of commuter operations meant that there was no chance of breaking even, let alone of returning a profit, so subsidies were required both for the replacement of obsolete equipment

ABOVE
Washington, D.C.'s Metrorail Metro Center station in 1976.

OPPOSITE
A Richmond Interurban car of 1909, otherwise known as car 1205.

OPPOSITE
The last run of the Chilliwack, Vancouver interurban cars, 30 September 1950, with cars 1310 and 1307 and motorman George Wolgemuth.

LEFT
Winter travel on the Montreal Rapid Transit System C in 1944.

Rapid rail car units running on the Chicago Transit Authority system in 1978.

and for the financial support of day-to-day operating costs. The first steps in addressing the problem came in the 1950s with moves toward the formation of regional transportation authorities, and the Urban Mass Transportation Act of 1964 opened the way for federal subsidies of two-thirds of the cost of approved schemes for the improvement of public transport. Toward the end of the 1960s the near collapse of many railroad operators, especially in the north-eastern part of the U.S.A., led to the Urban Mass Transportation Assistance Act of 1970, and this increased the provision of federal funds as well as guaranteeing the existing schemes for another decade.

The result was the creation of new

transport bodies in many cities. For example, the Metropolitan Transportation Authority covering the New York area assumed responsibility for the movement of more than 7 million people per day on its system of subways, buses and the main-line railroads of the bankrupt Penn-Central and Long Island Railroads, whose services were taken over by Conrail. Conrail also operated commuter services for the Boston, Connecticut, New Jersey and Philadelphia transport authorities, and from 1977 was committed by law to the operation of commuter services for any local authority prepared to provide the appropriate subsidies. Provision was also made for public transport authorities to purchase their own rolling stock and

track for operation by Conrail. This led to some extremely complicated services in which a number of bodies shared the ownership and also the operation of suburban passenger trains.

Over much the same period, renewed efforts were made to improve efficiency by the introduction of new equipment. One answer to the need for increased passenger capacity without the operation of more trains was the use of double-deck cars, as in most cases the limited length of the platforms at older stations prevented any increase in the length of trains. A number of railroads had introduced such cars from the early 1950s, and their use has become more common. Some of the first double-deck cars were introduced on the Chicago, Burlington & Quincy Railroad's suburban services during the late 1940s, when steam operation was still in force. The necessity of uncoupling locomotives and turning them round for the return journey at each end of the route was a long-standing nuisance on commuter services; but it has since been overcome by the use of diesel locomotion. Modern commuter trains are generally operated on the push-pull principle, with a driving cab at each end of the train. Some of these trains are in fixed sets, while others are arranged so that the length can be varied according to demand, thus avoiding the expense of running unnecessarily long trains outside rush hours.

Commuter services are generally reckoned to be those which operate between the city centre and points more than 20 miles (32km) distant, while the equivalent for short-distance transport is the rapid transit service, generally limited to the inner city area. Since these systems were built within the boundaries of established cities, they have often been forced underground in order to penetrate the busiest districts, although the first urban railway, the New York Elevated, adopted the other possible solution and was mounted on a raised platform. As early as 1867, a New York state committee investigating the transport needs of the city came to the conclusion that a system below the city's streets was the only immediate solution, but the same year saw the opening of the first section of elevated railway. Initial experiments with cable traction were soon discarded for steam locomotion. There were later a number of experiments with pneumatic power, but steam locomotion remained standard on the growing network of elevated lines until 1903, when electric traction became universal. By this time the first subways were under construction, and in 1904 came the inauguration of the first underground line, which ran just over 9 miles (14.5km) from City Hall via Grand Central Station to Times Square and Broadway at 145th Street. Subways and elevated railways were also built in Boston, Chicago, and Philadelphia at about the turn of the century, but it was some years before other cities followed suit.

Growing traffic congestion in more recent times has compelled other North

American cities to consider the adoption of rapid transit railways, but the enormous cost of tunnelling under city centres has resulted in large-scale official procrastination or a switch to the concept of the light rail system. Toronto and Montreal opened the first stages of expanding rapid transit systems in 1954 and 1966 respectively.

It was in the 1970s that American planners started to look to Europe for concepts concerning the means they could employ to rescue their cities from outward-spreading decay and the resultant economic decline. With urban transportation now owned by public bodies, the development of improved public transport could be undertaken with

a combination of city, state and national resources. This situation arrived at much the same time as the end of the American involvement in the Vietnam War, which meant that the military manufacturers were beginning to look for different markets to keep their production capabilities working at maximum profitability after the curtailment of military equipment spending, and decided that public transport would rapidly become the scene of considerable growth. An initial consequence of this situation was that Boston and San Francisco, two cities still operating tramway systems, contracted with Boeing-Vertol for the production of new LRVs (light rail vehicles) of the articulated type. These

A light rail vehicle at an underground station on San Francisco's municipal streetcar system in 1977.

With the name Amtrak displayed on its nose for everyone to see, a set of refurbished Metroliners speeds through Lanham, Maryland, on its way to New York from Washington, D.C. The high-speed trains offer hourly services in both directions between the two cities.

were based on a design schemed as the basis for an LRV which the company hoped would emulate the PCC of some 40 years earlier in becoming standard throughout the U.S.A. and also offering considerable export potential. The company's hopes were sound but its product was not, and the LRV was a disaster at the technical level as the company sought to 'reinvent the wheel' rather than learn from the wealth of experience available from practical operations elsewhere.

Thus it was in Canada that the first successful development of the new type of LRV emerged in North America, for it was here that the city of Edmonton decided that, rather than create a wholly new concept, it would draw on the experience of current European success. It therefore opted for the alternative approach of adapting European technology to the North American situation. The city thus constructed a new light rail line, partly on redundant railroad alignment and partly in city subways, and from 1978 used this for the operation of Siemens-Düwag trams imported from West Germany. The system was immediately successful, and as such was rapidly adopted as the model for San Diego in the U.S.A. and Calgary in Canada. In these two cities, it was decided that the creation of subways would be too expensive, so pedestrian and transit precincts were established in the city centres, it being rightly appreciated that trams, being guided

THE HISTORY OF NORTH AMERICAN RAIL

pollution-free vehicles, could be operated successfully and safely in areas otherwise reserved for pedestrians.

The success of these systems in attracting back to the use of public transit large numbers of motor car owners, who would never have considered the use of a bus, led to a considerable expansion in both the development and construction of light rail systems, and this has continued right up to the present. Major cities such as Baltimore, Buffalo, Dallas, Denver, Los Angeles, Portland, Sacramento and St. Louis have built new light rail lines, many of them as part of systems that are still expanding geographically and in scheduling to meet the demand engendered by their success. More recent examples of new and emerging systems are to be found in Jersey City and Salt Lake City, and progress toward similar systems has been made in other cities such as New York and Seattle. Moreover, the success of the concept persuaded cities such as Cleveland, Pittsburgh and Philadelphia, which operated systems based on the earlier streetcar concept, to

Trials of a light rail vehicle on San Francisco's municipal streetcar system.

OPPOSITE and LEFT
Locomotives await the call to duty at Amtrak's depot in Chicago, Illinois.

invest in the new type of rolling stock and begin a programme of expansion.

The example of Los Angeles is notably important, for this was an urban area that discarded its trams and intra-urbans during the 1960s in the belief that the city could live and breathe with the motor car. The dense pollution that has become a characteristic feature of Los Angeles finally proved to the city fathers that their predecessors were wholly wrong, and the city had inaugurated two new light rail lines, with a third already under construction.

Light rail first came into existence on the mainland of Europe in the form of new rolling stock and track segregated from public roadways to ensure that the

North and southbound trains pass on the elevated section of Washington, D.C.'s Metrorail Red Line, south of Rhode Island Avenue station.

services could maintain a high average speed. The pioneering concept of the European light rail system was derived largely from the planning which took place in the Swedish city of Gothenburg where, during a period of some 15 years, an ordinary city street tramway was extended through the suburbs, both new and existing, on high-speed reserved track, and every possible incentive was used to persuade the public to make extensive use of public transport. The existing rolling stock gave way to high-performance trams, and traffic restrictions were imposed to give priority to trams in the central area. This Swedish system was created without the cost of building tunnels, in the process not only minimizing cost but also keeping public transport on the surface as an attractive and readily-accessible system.

The concept of the light rail system is not of rigid definition, but in effect was conceived to accommodate all types of tracked transport in the gap between the bus and the heavy metro, or conventional railway, and can be operated like any of them. A light rail system is costlier to make than any bus system on city streets, but for a given capacity can be cheaper to operate, has lower whole-life costs, offers a higher average speed, produces less pollution, and in general is more successful in attracting motorists to public transport. In comparison with a metro or urban railway, a light rail system is cheaper to build and operate but functions at a lower speed. Among its other

Rapid-transit systems are light and relatively quiet, which makes it feasible for modern systems of this nature to be built above ground level in the U.S.A.'s most crowded cities. This speeds the construction process and also reduces the cost by a very considerable degree when compared with tunnelling.

The Monorail runs down 5th Avenue North as it leaves the Convention center in downtown Seattle.

LEFT
A southbound BART train just south of Fruitvale station in Oakland, California.

The rapid-transit system of San Diego, California, is based on the use of trams operating on carefully sited tracks through the centre of the city.

Passengers wait to shuttle round to key points in their city by means of a light rail system.

advantages, however, is the fact that it offers a visible example of successful public transport, provides better penetration of urban areas, is typified by better security, and generates less noise. Light rail can cater economically and effectively for passenger flows between 2,000 and 20,000 passengers an hour, and as a result is usually to be found in cities with populations between 200,000 and one million.

The light rail concept is usually based on the use of steel-wheeled vehicles running on steel rails and collecting electrical power from an overhead wire. Diesel light rail is a concept that has been evaluated to only a limited extent, and may prove to be useful for low-cost starter lines that can then be adapted to the full light rail concept. The steel rails can be grooved so that they lie flush with a street surface, or may be ballasted like normal railroad track, and this capability makes light rail the only system that can operate on both city streets and jointly with conventional rail services. It also offers the possibility of extending regional railroad

OPPOSITE
A PATH (Port Authority Trans-Hudson Corporation.) train comes over the river into Newark, New Jersey on a service from the World Trade Center in 1982.

LEFT
A Staten Island train in St. George station, by the Staten Island-New York Ferry terminus.

OPPOSITE
The use of double-deck cars allows the carriage of considerably larger numbers of passengers without any lengthening of the light rail train and, just as importantly, any linear extension of the platforms used by such services. This is a light rail station in San Bernardino, California.

LEFT
Passenger services are still of great importance for the movement of commuters to and from the major cities of the North American continent.

RIGHT and OPPOSITE
*Passenger services can
sometimes be thought of as
the Cinderella of the
American railroad system,
some services being operated
by elderly locomotives and
others by more advanced
locomotives fully integrated
with double-deck cars.*

services to the city centre by way of transfer points from rail to street track. Light rail is also very flexible in its applications, and can thus operate in a wide range of built-up environments. It can serve as a tramway in the street, though maximization of its advantages over the bus requires the minimization of unsegregated street track. Within public streets the track can be segregated by any of several means. The track can be laid in tarmac, concrete, ballast or even grass according to the operational and environmental needs of the whole system. Light rail can be built on previous railroad alignments, or indeed share track with the railroad in the form of little-used freight lines or those with limited passenger services, and technical progress means that the required safety arrangements are readily available for mixed services.

A topic closely related to the light rail revolution is the re-emergence of commuter trains, sometimes called heavy rail to differentiate it from light rail, as an important aspect of urban regeneration, for while the light rail system is dedicated to the rapid movement of people between various points in the urban environment, the commuter rail system has been re-established as the most cost-effective means of moving the workforce into the urban environment at the beginning of the working day and then returning the same people to their homes outside the city at night. The commuter train never wholly died in the U.S.A., but was severely strained by the rivalry of the private

motor car between the 1950s and 1980s and declined to a very low technical and commercial level.

In recent years, however, there has been a considerable renaissance in commuter operations in the U.S.A.'s major cities, and in a growing number of these conurbations the regional authorities have taken to operating what may be termed 'heavy rail' commuter services with their own trains running on track either acquired or leased from the railroad companies; in a number of other conurbations the regional authorities have contracted with the local railroad company for the operation of 'heavy rail' services.

In the area covered by the Connecticut Department of Transportation, for instance, a contract has been signed with Amtrak for the operation of a 50.6-mile (81.4-km) 'Shoreline East' commuter service between New London and New Haven via six intermediate stations. The service was launched in 1990 with two EMD F7M-class locomotives and Pullman-Standard cars dating from the 1950s and bought from the Port Authority of Allegheny County, Pittsburgh, following the latter's termination of its own commuter services. The Connecticut Department of Transportation has since expanded the operation by leasing from Guildford two GP38 and one GP7W-class power cars to haul 10 Bombardier Comet cars, supplemented by 11 existing Budd 8SPV200 railcars remodelled by Amtrak's Wilmington facility as standard cars.

At the start of 1996 the service was organized on the basis of peak-time schedules during the working week with two reciprocal runnings to ensure that the trains were positioned correctly for peak times. During 1996 the traffic carried increased by 6.5 per cent and, in anticipation of the high track speeds expected from Amtrak's forthcoming electrification of the line, an order was placed for six 3,000-hp (2237-kW) diesel locomotives to be manufactured by AMF Technotransport. The Connecticut Department of Transportation also controls (and with the New York Department of Transportation jointly subsidizes to the extent of 60 per cent of the operating deficit and 63 per cent of the capital cost) the commuter services operated by Metro-North between the city of New York and New Haven. The Connecticut Department of Transportation has also pressed the case for bus shuttles to its stations, thereby promoting reverse commuting, and such services now operate in Greenwich, New Haven, Norwalk and Stamford.

The Long Island Rail Road Company, which is a wholly owned subsidiary of the Metropolitan Transportation Authority, an agency of the State of New York, operates commuter services between the city of New York and destinations on Long Island, and operates within the limits of a budget allocated by the Metropolitan Transit Authority and includes sizeable elements of capital investment in new rolling stock, station improvements and

An urban scene typical of modern American commuter operations, in this instance at the Roosevelt Street station in Chicago.

An urban scene typical of modern American commuter operations, in this instance at the Roosevelt Street station in Chicago.

general infrastructure maintenance.

The extent and nature of the system's operations is revealed by the fact that in 1996 it carried 73.6 million passengers, and this was the fourth year in succession that their number had increased. However, in the first part of 1996 a reverse trend became evident, probably as a result of a fare increase of almost 10 per cent.

The Long Island Rail Road's services reach out into the Long Island counties of Nassau and Suffolk as well as to certain sections of the eastern Queens part of the New York conurbation. The services have nine branch lines that converge onto three main stations in New York, namely Penn Station, Flatbush Avenue in Brooklyn and Hunters Point Avenue that is open only at peak hours and is served only by diesel trains: the bulk of the daily traffic is handled by Penn Station, in the form of 208,000 passengers, the other two stations handling 40,000 passengers between them. It is worth noting that the Long Island Rail Road also handles a large quantity of freight services.

By the middle of the 1990s the Long Island Rail Road's programme to improve Pennsylvania Station was well under way, the $190 million programme having been designed to better the access to and the movement within the station, as well as to improve the station's facilities in terms of the level of comfort and information for the passengers. This effort is reflected in the fact that the average passenger now has 20 per cent more space and a 40 per cent increase in access points, the latter

An Amtrak passenger service passes through Jack London Square in Oakland, California.

A Metrolink service in San Bernardino, California.

including five stairways, three escalators, five elevators to Long Island Rail Road platforms, and even a new entrance. The importance attached to the attraction of commuter travellers back to the train (there are now 42 rather than the original 36 train movements per hour) is also revealed by general enhancements such as improvements to the signs and master destination boards, a new public address system, more effective lighting, and a traveller concourse with seats and washroom facilities.

The Long Island Rail Road began to receive new rolling stock in 1997–98, but up to that time operated a fleet of locomotives comprising 28 2,000-hp (1491-

kW) GP36-2-class, 23 1,500-hp (1119-kW) MP15AC-class and three FL9AC-class units as primary haulers, and also eight 1,000-hp (746-kW) SW1001 units for shunting operations. Passengers are carried in a fleet of 1,125 cars including 760 M1-class multiple-unit cars on the electrified inner suburban lines of the city of New York and in Nassau and Suffolk counties, and 174 examples of the M3-class car obtained in the mid-1980s. Operations to other parts of the network are handled by trains hauled by diesel-electric locomotives, which are scheduled for early replacement in the railroad's major reinvestment programme. The Long Island Rail Road also has an eye open to the use

of more flexible technology in the future, and is therefore evaluating dual-mode (diesel and third-rail electric) traction. The operator runs a single train in each direction during the peak-hour period between Penn Station and Port Jefferson on a non-electrified line using some of its 10 prototype double-deck cars obtained from Mitsui in Japan and powered by two FL9AC-class locomotives rebuilt to their current configuration by Adtranz, or ABB Traction as it then was.

It was in March 1995 that the Long Island Rail Road signed contracts worth some $250 million for new locomotives and passenger cars. The bulk of the contracts' value went to General Electric for 23 examples of its DE30AC-class diesel-electric locomotives for push/pull operations, as well as options for another 23 units that could be all of the same type or alternatively eight of the same type and 15 of a revised dual-mode type. The contracts also covered the manufacture and delivery of 48 new passenger cars. By this time, research had revealed that passengers had a decided preference for 2+2 seating rather than the 2+3 arrangement typical of the 10 prototype cars that had been initially evaluated over a two-year period with maximum accommodation for 180 passengers. The order therefore comprises cars with provision for a maximum of 145 passengers, reduced to 139 passengers in cab cars.

Farther to the south along the eastern seaboard of the U.S.A. is the area covered

A modern commuter train at Breakneck Ridge.

RIGHT
*The station at San
Bernardino, California.*

OPPOSITE
*An Amtrak passenger
service at Pinole.*

by the Maryland Mass Transit Administration's Maryland Rail Commuter Service. This provides services over the 75.6-mile (121.6-km) route linking Washington, D.C. and Perryville via Baltimore on electrified track within the context of Amtrak's 'North-East Corridor' operation, a 37.9-mile (61-km) route linking Washington, D.C. and Baltimore on non-electrified track, and a 72.6-mile (116.8-km) route linking Washington, D.C. and Martinsburg on non-electrified track.

The service between Washington, D.C. and Perryville is the responsibility of four electric locomotives hauling Japanese-built passenger cars, while the services on the other two routes are operated with older stock using diesel locomotives.

During 1994 the Maryland Rail Commuter Service posted a total annual passenger figure of some 5 millions which, at 6 per cent over the previous year, seemed to indicate a levelling off of growth from the 20 per cent figure evident

in previous years. Operating within the context of the Maryland Mass Transit Authority, the Maryland Rail Commuter Service is able to offer tickets and passes valid throughout the system and this is clearly a decided inducement to passengers to use all aspects of the service, which include the bus, light rail and metro services of Baltimore and, it is hoped for the near future, Washington, D.C. The Maryland Rail Commuter Service is growing slightly with the aid of a federal

LIGHT RAIL & RAPID TRANSIT SYSTEMS

financial package that is allowing a 13.4-mile (21.6-km) extension to Frederick with the aid of new track, signalling equipment, rolling stock etc. Further evidence of the integrated nature of the Maryland Mass Transit Administration is provided by the Maryland Rail Commuter Service's completion of a new station at Dorsey, which has a major parking capability and its own links to the Maryland state highway system.

The Maryland Rail Commuter Service's train equipment comprises four AEM7-class electric locomotives and 25 3,000-hp (2238-kW) GP40WH-2-class locomotives together with more than 100 passengers cars in the form of 43 refurbished New Jersey Transit Authority and 63 new Sumitomo cars, complemented in due course by 50 double-deck cars ordered in 1995 from Kawasaki.

Located farther to the north, around Boston, the Massachusetts Bay Transportation Authority provides commuter rail services on 11 routes into Boston on a network comprising 308.1 miles (495.9 km) of track originally owned up to the 1970s by Penn-Central and Boston & Maine. From 1988 the Massachusetts Bay Transportation Authority's sphere of influence was extended by the inauguration of a service to Providence, Rhode Island, on Amtrak tracks. All of the Massachusetts Bay Transportation Authority's services are operated under contract by Amtrak.

The Massachusetts Bay Transportation

Authority controls an integrated and comprehensive local and regional transportation system based on four metro lines, five light rail lines, four trolley bus and 155 bus routes all operating within the same basic fare system to encourage interconnection between various elements of the overall system, which also included the heavy rail commuter system. In 1995 the Massachusetts Bay Transportation Authority recorded a passenger total of 23 million, and further expansion of the commuter service is imminent from the inauguration of a 22.9-mile (36.8-km) extension from Framingham to Worcester on the western side of the network south of the line to Fitchburg, and from the start in the later 1990s of *Old Colony* railroad services along three routes to Kingston, Middleboro and Scituate to the south-east of Boston and including 21 new stations. These latter extensions of the network are estimated to result in the delivery of up to 15,000 more passengers per day to the South Station in Boston. The success of the Massachusetts Bay Transportation Authority in schedule keeping, fare management and general efficiency has led to the local decision to consider other extensions to the route network to both the north and south of Boston, including coastal destinations such as Newburyport and Greenbush.

The Massachusetts Bay Transportation Authority operates its services with 58 diesel locomotives and 420 passenger cars. The diesel locomotives include 25 F40PH-2C, bought from General Motors, and 18

F40PH and 12 F40PH-2M-class units rebuilt to an improved standard by Morrison Knudsen. Further capability is being provided, largely for the Worcester and *Old Colony* services, by the delivery of 25 more locomotives remanufactured to an upgraded standard by AMF Technotransport. The passenger cars are of mixed origins, and include 67 units made by Messerschmitt-Bölkow-Blohm in West Germany, 147 units fabricated by Bombardier in Canada, 92 double-deck units constructed by Kawasaki in Japan, and 58 Pullman-Standard units originally made in the U.S.A. and now upgraded.

Much farther to the west, Metra is the name of the commuter branch of the Chicago Regional Transportation Authority under the overall supervision of North-East Illinois Regional Commuter Railroad Corporation's Chicago Commuter Rail Service Board, this mass of nomenclature finally revealing that Metra is in fact the organization that operates commuter rail services to and from the Chicago conurbation. The Metra system covers the six north-eastern counties of Illinois, and its extent of some 500 miles (805km) of route (including 1,200 miles/1930km of track) includes elements operated under contract by the Burlington Northern Santa Fe Railroad (originally the Burlington Northern Railroad, one route) and the Union Pacific Railroad (formerly the Chicago & North Western Railroad, three routes) on their own track but with Metra-owned equipment. Owned and operated by Metra itself are the track and

equipment of the former Illinois Central, Milwaukee Road and Rock Island Railroads, and Metra has also leased the Norfolk Southern line to Orland Park for its South-West Service. Metra additionally operates two *Central Heritage Corridor* services in each direction between Chicago and Joliet.

During August 1998 Metra introduced a commuter service to the 52.8-mile (85-km) Wisconsin Central route linking Franklin Park (on Metra's own route between Chicago and Elgin) and Antioch via nine intermediate stations. Further extensions of the system are under active consideration.

Metra's rolling stock in the closing stages of 1995 included 137 diesel locomotives, 165 electric railcars and 700 passenger cars. The most important of the diesel locomotives were 28 3,200-hp (2386-kW) F40P-class, 86 3,200-hp (2386-kW) F40PH-2 class, 15 3,200-hp (2386-kW) F40C-class and 30 3,200-hp (2386-kW) F40PHM-2-class units, while the most important types of electric railcar were the 150-passenger MA3A class of which 130 were in service and the 150-passenger MA3B class of which 35 were in service. Entering service since 1994 have been a number of 'highliner' electric multiple-unit cars after their reconstruction with full accessibility to physically handicapped passengers by Morrison Knudsen and later by Amerail.

Back on the east coast between Massachusetts and Maryland is the state of New Jersey, and this is the area of

commuter train responsibility exercised by the organization known as New Jersey Transit Rail Operations Inc., which carries an annual total of some 42.7 million passengers over a system that comprises nine routes into Hoboken, Newark and the city of New York, and is operated with an integrated fare system to facilitate interchange within the various elements of the whole complex. Within this complex New Jersey Transit Rail Operations owns much of the infrastructure (the other parts being in the hands of Amtrak and Conrail), all its own rolling stock and 145 stations.

The system operates some 600 services on every day of the working week, and these services fall into several distinct sectors. On the Jersey Coast line between Penn Station in New York and Bay Head there are *Jersey Arrow* services operated by electric multiple-units as far south as Long Branch, and also diesel-hauled services as far as Bay Head. On the North-East Corridor from Penn Station to Trenton (and including the branch line to Princeton) there is another *Arrow* service also operated by electric multiple-units. From Newark extends the line into the Raritan Valley as far as Hackettstown, operated by General Motors electric units, while the Morris and Essex lines are generally operated by electric multiple-units together with a number of diesel-hauled trains. Diesel services are standard on the services to Boonton, the Pascack Valley and Port Jervis, and the link to Atlantic City via

OPPOSITE
Southern Pacific No. 3207 waits with the commuter train to San Jose. Train 142 has one single- and two double-deck coaches.

LEFT
An Amtrak service passes through Jack London Square in Oakland, California.

Philadelphia is served by a fleet of five diesel locomotives and 18 passenger cars.

At the end of 1995 New Jersey Transit Rail Operations had 78 diesel-electric and 28 electric locomotives together with 300 electric multiple-units and 389 passenger cars. The most numerous of the diesel-electric units were 13 3,000-hp (2238-kW) GP40PH-2 class and 40 3,000-hp (2238-kW) F40PH-2-class locomotives, the electric locomotives were 20 5,795-hp (4320-kW) ALP44 and eight 6,000-hp (4475-kW) E60CP-class units, and the primary electric multiple-units were 68 MA1G-class units in married pairs, 182 MA1J-class units in married pairs and 29 MA1J-class units in single cars. Recent additions have included another 17 ALP44-class electric locomotives to replace E60CP units, and the first Bombardier cars to replace older MA1G-class electric multiple-units.

On the other side of the U.S.A., operating in the extreme south of California on the west coast, is the North San Diego County Transit Development Board, which in 1995 started the *Coaster* service operated under contract by Amtrak over the 41.75-mile (67.2-km) route linking San Diego and Oceanside. This service runs over part of the 83.3 miles (134km) of route that the North San Diego County Transit Authority bought from the Burlington Northern Santa Fe Railroad and includes the branch line between Oceanside and Escondido which is under consideration for a light rail service. The North San Diego County Transit Development Board has upgraded the route of the *Coaster* service in a number of ways, including six new stations and two upgraded stations, and for its service (comprising five trains to/from San Diego and one train to/from Oceanside in the morning and evening of each day of the working week) five F40PHM-2C-class diesel-electric locomotives and 16 double-deck coaches (eight cab cars and eight passenger cars) supplied by Bombardier and being supplemented by another five coaches.

Farther to the north along the Californian coast is the region operated by the Southern California Regional Rail Authority in and around the Los Angeles conurbation. It is planned that this system will eventually cover some 400 miles (645km), and the first three lines came into service during October 1992 after the Southern California Regional Rail Authority had purchased 338 miles (544km) of route from the Burlington Northern Santa Fe Railroad as the beginning of a programme designed to bring effective commuter services to five counties in the Los Angeles region. The services introduced in 1992 operated under the designation 'Metrolink', and comprised the routes linking the Union Station in Los Angeles with Moorpark (the Ventura Line), Montclair (the San Bernardino Line), and Santa Clarita (the Santa Clarita Line), and two services added in 1995 were the Riverside Line on Union Pacific track and the Orange County Line, the latter extending to Oceanside and a link with service to San Diego. Further expansion came in October 1995 when the Metrolink network was extended to include the route between Irvine and Riverside via Santa Ana and Anaheim, so by the beginning of 1996 the Metrolink network comprised 338 miles (544km) of route with 42 stations, and during its first three years of service the Metrolink carried steadily increasing numbers of passengers, peaking in the year up to October 1995 at 4,4 million, a 33 per cent increase over the previous 12-month period.

The Metrolink services are operated by Amtrak, as noted above, using 23 F59PH class and eight F59PHI-class locomotives optimized for the type of low emissions now considered absolutely vital for all traffic operating in the heavily polluted Los Angeles basic, and 94 double-deck passengers cars delivered by Bombardier. The operator was also to have received 26 special 'California Cars' ordered from Morrison Knudsen, but the order for these commuter cars was later cancelled because of manufacturing problems, and Metrolink instead leased more Bombardier cars from GO Transit of Canada.

There are several other commuter or 'heavy rail' operators in the USA filling the specialized niche between the 'light rail' systems of the city centres and the main-line services still running passenger and freight services between the USA's main centres of population, but the above pen picture provides an encapsulated view of the overall nature of such services in the U.S.A.

As illustrated here, in this photograph of the shoreline of the lake at Klamath Falls, Oregon, the lifeblood of American surface transportation is provided by the road and the railroad track, running in parallel with one another.

Picture Acknowledgements

Military Archive & Research Services, Lincolnshire, England: back cover, pages 2, 14 top left and below right, 17 top, 20 left, 23, 29, 32, 34, 37, 38, 39 both, 40 both, 41, 42, 52, 53, 54, 56 both, 59, 73, 82, 86 right, 87, 88 below, 89 below, 91, 97 both, 100, 102 below, 109, 111, 115, 117 both, 119, 123 top, 135, 139, 149 below, 152, 154 below, 171, 173 top 176, 180, 183 both, 200 top and below right, 218 both, 219, 222, 232 top and below right, 233 both, 244, 246, 247, 324 both, 329 both, 340, 341, 342, 343, 344, 347, 349, 354, 355, 362, 363, 364, 365, 366, 368, 369, 370, 371, 374, 382, 386, 387 both, 393, 395, 403, 404, 405, 406, 407, 408
*American Locomotive Company:** page 17 below
*Association of American Railroads, U.S.A.:** pages 9, 11, 13 both, 14 left, 15 top right, 19, 20 right, 43, 51
*AT&SF Railway:** pages 79, 351, 373
*Baltimore & Ohio Railroads Museum:** pages 15 below left, 18 top, 21, 30, 48 right, 81, 88 top, 95 below, 157, 172, 173 below, 177, 181, 187, 350
*Boeing Vertol Company, Philadelphia, U.S.A.:** page 409
*Burlington Northern Photo:** pages 64, 70, 103, 161 right, 162, 163
*Canadian National:** pages 192, 193 below right, 194 top, 223, 340
*Canadian Pacific:** pages 193 top and below left, 195 right, 212 right, 245, 247
*Chicago & North Western Railway:** page 334 below
*Chicago, Burlington & Quincy:** pages 35, 47, 99, 144, 148
*Delaware & Hudson Railroad, U.S.A.:** page 14 right
*Denver & Rio Grande Western Railroad:** page 122-3 below
*Frye, Harry A. New Hampshire:** page 122 top
*Gulf Oil Company:** page 10
*Great Northern Railway:** pages 149 top right, 164 top, 167, 328 top
*Illinois Central Railroad:** pages 18 below, 27 below, 102 top
*Jennifer Moore Personality Picture Library, London:** page 86 left
*Lehigh Valley Railroad:** page 134
*Library of Congress:** pages 69, 96
*Milwaukee Public Library:** page 138
*Milwaukee Road Collection:** pages 48 left, 136, 141
*Missouri Pacific Railroad:** pages 85, 278 above
*The National Archives Division of Photographic Archives & Research:** page 36
*New York Central Railroad:** page 140
*Norfolk & Western Railway Co. Virginia:** pages 127 below, 137
*Northern Pacific:** pages 71, 75, 89 top, 90, 94, 151, 166, 174 both, 334 above
*NY City Transit Authority:** page 118
*Personality Pictures Library, London:** page 68
*Pullman Company:** page 345
©**Railfotos, Millbrook House Limited, Oldbury, W. Midlands, England:** front cover, title page, pages 4, 12, 16, 24, 26, 27 top, 63, 65, 66-67, 72, 74, 84 both, 93, 95 top, 98, 101, 105, 106, 107, 112, 116, 120, 121, 124, 125, 128, 129, 145, 146, 147, 150, 153, 154 top, 156, 158, 159, 160 both, 165, 168, 169, 170, 178, 179, 182, 191, 194

below, 195 left, 196 both, 197, 198, 199, 200 left, 201 both, 202, 203, 204, 205, 210 both, 211, 216 all, 217, 206, 207, 208, 209, 212 left, 213, 214, 215, 220, 221, 224, 225, 226 both, 227, 228, 229, 230, 231, 234 both, 235, 236, 237, 238, 239, 240-241, 242 both, 243, 248, 249, 250, 251, 252, 253, 254, 255 both, 256, 257, 258, 259, 260, 261, 262, 263, 264, 265, 266, 267, 268, 269, 270, 273, 274, 275, 276, 277, 279 top right and below left, 280, 281, 282, 283, 284, 285, 286 both, 287, 288, 289, 290, 291, 292, 293, 294, 295, 296, 297, 298, 299, 300, 301, 302, 303, 304, 305, 306 both, 307, 308 both, 309, 310, 311, 312, 313, 314, 315, 316, 317, 318, 319, 320, 321, 322, 323, 325, 326 both, 327, 328 below, 330, 331 both, 332, 333, 335, 338, 339 both, 353, 356, 356, 358, 359, 360, 361, 367, 372, 376, 378, 379, 380, 381, 383, 384, 385, 388, 389, 390, 392, 396, 397, 398, 400, 401, 402, 410, 411, 413, 414, 415, 416, 417, 418, 419, 420, 421, 422, 433, 424, 425, 426, 427, 428, 429, 430, 431, 433, 434, 435, 437
*Santa Fe Railway Photo:** pages 50, 78 both, 83, 104, 126, 130 top, 131, 133, 164 below, 184, 188, 189, 278 below, 279 below right, 336, 342, 377
*Southern Pacific Company:** pages 55, 77 right
*Southern Pacific Railroad:** pages 142, 175, 391
*Thomas Golcrease Inst.:** page 49
*Toronto Transit Commission:** page 232 left
*Union Pacific Railroad Museum, Nebraska:** pages 46, 61, 76, 92, 127 top, 130 below, 132, 143, 149 top left, 185, 279 top left, 341, 343, 346, 348, 352
*United Pacific Railroad Museum:** pages 44, 45, 80
*U.S. National Archives:** page 114
*U.S. Signal Corps:** pages 57, 155
*Vanderbilt University, U.S.A.:** page 60
*WMATA/P Myatt:** page 412
*York County Historical Society:** page 6

Prints/transparencies through Military Archive & Research Services, Lincolnshire, England.